Praise for

Peace of Mind

- PATHWAYS TO SUCCESSFUL LIVING -

By Sue Washington

"**Peace of Mind™** is a wonderful pack. It is a veritable cornucopia of therapeutic and philosophical advice on how to enhance our wellbeing. It is presented in the form of a workbook, with chapters containing clear and highly practical steps designed to guide us away from angst and despair and towards calmer, more fulfilling lives.

Sue Washington infuses her writing with a remarkable combination of knowledge, skill, experience, humour and - above all - wisdom. I heartily recommend **Peace of Mind™**, not only as a source of inspiration to those whose find themselves lost in a dark wood, but also to those hoping to guide them back into the light".

Professor Chris Dowrick, MD, Professor of Primary Medical Care, University of Liverpool.

"I did the Peace of Mind training in 1994 to help me with my personal development. This course led me on a voyage of discovery that changed my life and way of thinking about others and myself. I now work in the field of Referral Marketing, helping others achieve their goals and sharing the skills first developed through Peace of Mind.

My business is now turning over £3,000,000, per annum and thousands of families are now benefiting from additional income through my business. My income is considerable, and I now earn more in a month than I did in a year".

Ray Cranston, Newcastle-upon-Tyne.

"I just wanted to let you know how much completing your Peace of Mind™ course has changed my life. Changes have been achieved and the way I think and act has been altered for the better; my confidence, self esteem and health have all improved and I find it much easier to be positive about life in general. Things are going very well for me.

Thank you for everything you have taught and shown me. It has helped me grow as a person and I hope that my growth will now continue for the rest of my life. I feel like you have given me an enormous gift and words are not enough to express the gratitude I feel. Long may your courses continue, I think as many people as possible should attend, if not for re-training then for their own personal development. Thank you again".

Sue Senior, Wantage, Oxfordshire

"I began training with **Peace of Mind**™ when I was a foster mother and looking for solutions to help me deal with disturbed children in my care. I also realised I had to deal with my own reactions to their behaviour. When I met Sue Washington, I was very impressed by her calmness and caring attitude, and I knew I had made the right decision.

The course was tough in some ways, but it was the best thing I ever did. It enabled me to take charge of my life!"

Irene Jamieson, Inverness

"I wish to testify to the value and benefits which I believe I obtained from completion of the **Peace of Mind**™ programme. I undertook the programme in 1994 when I was in the process of considering the opening of my own psychological practice, and seeking to enhance my professional skills and obtain practical advice on undertaking such an entrepreneurial initiative.

——   The training was highly successful … the programme firstly was effective in challenging taken-for-granted professional beliefs and practices regarding client interaction, support and evaluation, an essential component in promoting professional growth.   The programme has extended my own professional competence.

Judging by client evaluations and increased demand for my services, the confidence inculcated by the content of the programme and the skills of the trainers has substantially enhanced my ability to offer a range of psychological and therapeutic support of perceived value to children, young people, adults and organisations within the community".

Dr. Jack Tollan, Troon, Scotland

"The module as it stands, has gone extremely well with our existing clientele, and I'd like to market it more strongly to schools, and so on, to build on this success"

John Lathom, Head of In-Service Education,
Liverpool John Moores University.

"Without exception, **Peace of Mind**™ has been appreciated and valued by all participating"

Dorothy Mitchell, Rossendale Hospice, Lancashire

"October 1997 was a turning point in my life, when I joined **Peace of Mind**™ training. I now accept that I am a good enough wife, mum, & deputy, and that I have always done my best. I understand how easily I fell into 'taking on' the problems of others - I encouraged dependency, and deprived others of a sense of achievement coming from sorting out their own problems. I was stifling staff with care perhaps to the point of teachers participating in "learned helplessness" (Seligman 1975) a condition where people are exposed to uncontrollable aversive events for long periods, eventually give up trying to master the situation, become passive, and stop trying to influence their fate".

Deputy Head Teacher, Merseyside

"Having taken up the **Peace of Mind**™ course as part of my ongoing professional development, I was unprepared for the immensely positive effect it would have on both my work life and family life. As a therapist it has given me so many useful techniques with which I can help my clients & improve my ability to communicate with others. But surprisingly even within my family life, my ability to listen and communicate with my children has been greatly improved, and I am even managing to get my own way (occasionally)!!"

Anne Millne-Riley, Therapist and Mother

"I can confidently recommend Sue Washington's **Peace of Mind**™ Pack to any student or young teacher. It is full of sound practical advice from one who is both an excellent teacher and an experienced psychotherapist

Some time ago I introduced this pack to a young student who was about to start a teacher-training course, and had some misgivings about her lack of teaching practice. Now in her second year at college she tells me how valuable Sue's sensible advice has been".

Mr. H.Les George, OBE, retired Head teacher

"Sue Washington's publication "Peace of Mind" is a tremendous piece of literary genius, and an essential reference work for any practitioner member of either the Conventional or Complementary Healing Professions.

Most of us who see clients or patients on a day to day basis will identify with the many useful pointers included in the book, which can only be of benefit for all concerned.

I would thoroughly recommend it to fellow practitioners, and certainly those utilizing homeopathic therapy where the mind is such an important consideration in the prescription".

Ken Atherton
NHS Healthcare Professional/Registered Homeopath
Member of the Department of Health Steering Group for the Regulation of
Acupuncture, Herbal, Chinese Herbal & Traditional Medicines.

"I've popped in to tell you I feel MUCH better. I'm not being so hard on myself, and I've only just started the distance learning programme".

Jeanne Evans, Preston, Lancashire

"Refreshing, comprehensive, intensive, a gift for life. This course is not (just) academic, I lived it: more rewarding than any other course of study I've ever undertaken".

Denise Ashurst, Liverpool.

Sue, I wanted to write to thank you for the wonderful material I have used from this book. Since being a trainee, I have been putting into practice the things I learned in my personal, then in my professional life as a therapist also, and in turn passed this on to others exponentially. By passing on techniques in this way I have now had feedback from many, many people over these almost ten years, saying how they have transformed themselves also. Thank you so much.

Now you have found a way of getting to an even larger audience. I hope with all my heart that some have the sense to pick up the techniques and run with them and that you get the recognition you deserve.

Vicki Rebecca BA, Holistic Therapist, Aberdeen.

"Peace of Mind sets out a sound approach to building self-esteem for those who read it and use it to strengthen practice. This enhanced self - and practitioner - esteem sets the foundation for other avenues explored in the text. As a past recipient and practitioner of the positive values encapsulated in the peace of mind training I would have no hesitation in recommending this integrated book and workbook.

Peace of Mind™ is a much needed addition to a market that varies form the intense academic to the somewhat bizzare! It makes accessible an approach to change that is refreshingly meaningful".

Dr Patricia Mullins, Reader in Education
Liverpool John Moores University

General comments

"It enabled me to take charge of my life, instead of letting other people make decisions for me".

"My new confidence led me to taking Open University courses, getting my degree and transforming my life in many ways.

"I have found a great deal of happiness resulting from the way I now conduct my life. I would thoroughly recommend **Peace of Mind**™ training to anyone who feels they are missing something, but can't quite find it".

"It helps you to find yourself".

Peace of Mind

- PATHWAYS TO SUCCESSFUL LIVING -

By Sue Washington

An integrated book and workbook

Mnemodynamics Unlimited, 145 Chapel Lane, Longton, Preston,
PR4 5NA.

A record of this book is lodged with the UK Copyright Service

ISBN 978-0-9559263-0-3

Printed and bound in Great Britain by Lightning Source UK Limited,
Milton Keynes.

Acknowledgements

A big thank you to Peter Blythe who introduced me to the field of Psychotherapy in 1968. To Dr Fran Renwick, for her brilliant writing skills, constant support and the enlightening moment when she said 'This deserves to be published'. To Ivan Sokolov and Jacquie Pearson who changed my life as a single parent by showing me many of the skills which I now pass on to you within this volume. To Margaret Middleton for telling me about the "Trimtab factor" and David Middleton for constant wisdom and clarity. Thanks also to Dr Pat Mullins from Liverpool John Moores University who personally gained from this material, and believed in it so much that she wanted to make it part of mainstream education. She helped got the **Peace of Mind**™ package to become a module in the MA in Education at LJMU where it has run for several years. Both school staff and pupils seem to have benefited from this work as teachers picked it up and used the skills. To Adrienne and George Green who made the metaphor which is the Prologue of the book. It is a wonderful compliment, thank you.

Thank you to the people who have read this volume and made comment: Denise Ashurst, Ken Atherton, Ray Cranston, Professor Christopher Dowrick, Jeanne Evans, Mr Les George OBE, Irene Jamieson, John Lathom, Anne Millne-Riley, Dorothy Mitchell, Dr. Pat Mullins, Vicki Rebecca, Sue Senior and Dr. Jack Tollan

Thanks also to John & Lynn Quigley for encouragement and guidance and my friends and colleagues and clients who have taught me so much. Many are mentioned within. Thank you to Benedict Chieffo, my son who let me try out so many of the techniques that are given within this book, and was the originator of the **Peace of Mind**™ model the day he said to me, some fifteen years ago 'How did you know what to teach me, Mum?' It's a good moment when you realise to yourself as a parent 'Here is a nice person'. I am proud to know you, my son. As well as all that, in later years he lent technical support after gaining his degree in IT. Lastly, but by no means least of all, to Don Hatherley, my husband and friend who has always been there for me.

Dedication

For my parents George and Jeanne Washington, who always did their
best, and for my son Ben Chieffo, who is the best of me.

I want to be in a happy relationship

Contents

Prologue: The Girl with No Clothes Sense

Once upon a time there was a girl who had No Clothes Sense. She knew that she had No Clothes Sense because when she looked around she saw lots of people looking beautiful and self-assured in colourful new clothes. Sometimes she tried to dress colourfully too, but somehow the effect never seemed to be quite the same. So she carried on wearing the same dull old things that she always wore, and tried not to care about having No Clothes Sense and never being colourful, but she often felt sad and disorganised without quite knowing why.

One day she met a woman who looked right into her eyes and smiled at her and exclaimed, "Oh, aren't you pretty!" When the girl heard this she looked around to see who the woman was talking to, but there was no one else nearby. So she said "I'm sorry, who do you mean? You can't be talking to me. I have No Clothes Sense, everyone knows that." The woman didn't say anything, but just smiled again, and the girl found herself smiling back and the sad feeling seemed to go away for a while.

The next day the girl found herself trying on some new clothes, and even though she had No Clothes Sense, the woman laughed and threw her arms around her because she looked so pretty. The next day, and the next, and the one after that the girl tried on more new things, and each day the sad feeling became a little fainter and her life became a little calmer and more organised, and each day the girl worried less and less about having No Clothes Sense.

Then one day the girl was walking down the street hardly feeling sad at all and she saw a shadow in a doorway. Then she realised that it wasn't a shadow at all but a small grey person. "Hello," said the girl. The small grey person looked surprised. "There's no point in talking to me," she said. "I have No Clothes Sense, everyone knows that." The girl looked at the small grey person and she felt a smile starting from deep inside her. The smile grew and grew until it burst out onto her face, so bright that it lit up the small grey person so brightly that she had to smile too. "My," said the girl, smiling like the sun and holding out a hand. "Aren't you pretty?"

Part I: Building Understanding

1

Choice or Reaction

As we look at the world around us, we don't have to have special powers of deduction to work out that 'things' are not going quite as well as they ought.   Words such as "unemployment", "homelessness", "crime rate", "war", "social unrest", "pollution", "AIDS", "cancer", "allergies" and many more indicate our social climate. People are turning this way and that for solutions, and spending vast sums of money on 'wonder-cures' to heal body, mind or bank balance.

Amid this hubbub of fear and negativity, a few small voices are reminding us that our lives are intertwined, and everything we do spreads out like ripples, affecting the world and other lives in ways we can hardly imagine. The body of evidence linking our mental or emotional state and our physical well-being is so overwhelming that we finally begin to see that something in our lives other than 'bad luck' may be the cause of our eczema, depression or migraine headaches. Slowly we begin to realise that recycling papers or bottles may indeed have an effect, and some of us begin to ask what *else* can we do?

Looking around and not liking what we see - we begin to wonder about the truth in the old sales slogan: *'if you always do what you always did, you always get what you always got'.* If you are asking, *'So what else can I do?'* and if you, like many people, have begun to realise that while it is true that our *actions* affect the world around us, it is our *thoughts* and our *attitudes* that produce these actions, then these words are for you. I dedicate this book to the healing of the pain that lies beneath the attitudes that allow us to hurt one another and the world around us.   Perhaps together we can discover that we all have a 'wonderful dress sense', and that by helping to spread a little bit more **Peace of Mind** we can begin a ripple effect that will restore colour to our world.

Model of the Mind

We spend many years in formal education, learning the appropriate use of our minds. We learn social interaction by trial and error, and by feedback from our families, friends and society in general. The little we do learn about our feelings and how to deal with them is governed by general assumptions and stereotypes such as, "boys don't cry", or, "girls like pink".

We don't learn how to deal with the rage we sometimes feel towards our parents when we are children or teenagers, or how to deal with feelings of jealousy towards a younger brother or sister who appears to have what we want. Parents, never having had help dealing with these issues themselves are unlikely to know what to do for their children. Generation after generation of us end up feeling uncomfortable and incompetent when faced with the emotions of others.

"Don't be silly, there's nothing to be scared of!"
"Stop crying, it's only a little scratch!"
"Don't be angry!"
"Calm down!"
"That's nothing - when I was a lad ...."

How often do words like these, and many more besides echo down the generations. Each time words like this are used by a parent or someone important in our lives, it invalidates the way we feel and a little part of us begins to doubt ourselves and our ability to know ourselves. We begin to think that we must be wrong and these other voices must be right, but still we feel what we feel. The hurt still hurts and the anger or frustration still smoulders, but it becomes easier to hide it away, to store it somewhere where it doesn't bother us.

Because of the way we have been labelled in the past, negatively or positively, we build up an image of ourselves as the, "clever" or "strong" or "clumsy" or "stupid" person suggested by our world. Everything that disagrees with that picture gets pushed away and stored or denied so that we don't know it ever existed.

We may carry on like this for years or in some cases for our whole lives, no longer knowing what we feel or who we are, dutifully believing what we were told, perhaps decades ago. Until 'something' happens! Perhaps one day we are faced with the distressed cries of a hurt child, and these cries reverberate deep inside, and suddenly we hear the cries of the small child we locked away all those years ago by not believing its hurt - the small child we once were. In that instant we experience not only the pain of the time we hurt ourselves and were not acknowledged, but also the pain of all the tears of hurt that we shed throughout our lives, from all the times we felt ignored or insignificant.

Overwhelmed by this unexpected wave of emotion, we know we need to shut it off quickly. So we turn to the reason for the way we feel now - the crying child in front of us. We shush the child, just as we were shushed, or smack the child as we were smacked. We know it's the only way, that it's for the child's own good, just as it was for ours. We do the best we can, just as our parents before us did the best they could at the time. And we try to push our uncomfortable or distressing feeling back under lock and key in our storage system.

There are many different events that can trigger a response from our storage system. Sometimes we recognise these times retrospectively, when we realise that we have over-reacted in some way and dumped a huge load of anger, sadness, or some other emotion onto a relatively minor incident. Our storage system is vastly complex, but has a certain logic to it - the logic of association.

Jane

A very lovely twenty-four year old woman came to see me for the second time. At her first session a week earlier, she described how she was feeling overwhelmingly rejected. She and her fiancée had parted company some five months previously, but even after the lapse of time to the appointment day, her feelings had not subsided one jot. Whilst the two had been reasonably close, it seemed to her that her still-strong reaction was a little over the top. I listened to her "story". As a twelve-year-old, and the youngest of four daughters, her mother died. Her first thought was "How can she leave me?" This was followed by feelings which she listed as: "shocked, very upset, gutted, had a pain in the stomach, helpless, powerless" (and wait for it -) "rejected; wants to die too; (and) guilty about leaving the rest of the family should she take this course of action".

We worked together with these feelings in a variety of psychotherapeutic ways (using a therapy called Mnemodynamic Therapy) leaving her image of that same little girl, by the end of the session "relieved". I knew she would feel better by the next session, not because I said so, though I did, but because **she** *said so. "Relieved" was how she'd left the image of herself. At the start of the second session my young woman looked wonderful, wholesome, and with a glow about her. I asked "On a scale of nought to ten (not that anyone's at nought, but if you had been when you last came to me, and ten is "wellness"), where are you up to?*

"Seven" was her immediate reply. "Brilliant" I thought. How hard she had worked. That night she dealt with two incidents. The first was when she was fourteen. Her father had a row with an older sister, who was then thrown out of the house. Her feelings were: "very upset, stranded, trapped, helpless, powerless, anger and resentment to father, furious, enraged, murderous". She worked with those feelings, and left the younger person "comforted".

EXERCISE 1

ACCEPTING FEELINGS
(Allow 10 or 15 minutes to do this exercise)

Remember a time as a child or teenager when you told your parents how you were feeling and got a response from them something like - 'Don't be silly darling it's not that bad'.

1.   Please write down how you felt in such circumstances.

(There are people who will not like any process that involves instructions on pieces of paper – it can remind them too much of school experiences best forgotten. It is my intention to help you help yourself just as much as you can. Please do the best you know how with all the exercises in boxes throughout the book).

2.   What would you have liked to have heard or experienced instead?

This exercise has been done many times before in **Peace of Mind** Training groups. When you have finished your list, it may be helpful for you to look at what you as a person actually needed.

Let me guess a word or two that may well have come up:

> Acknowledgement?

> Validation?

> Time?

> Acceptance?

These words are ones that come up time and again in groups. Most of us will find at this point that we did not get the acceptance we wanted from the significant people around us. Your list will probably include feelings like acknowledgement, validation, to feel cared about, to be heard, to be loved, to be given time and so on.

It is too late to turn the clock back and alter those past situations. I urge you to act NOW to redress the balance in the needs that you list - that is: -

> Acknowledge YOURSELF.

> Validate YOURSELF.

> Give YOURSELF time.

> Accept YOURSELF.

It would seem that many of us need the same kinds of acknowledgements much of the time!

After that, we moved to another incident, the parting of the ways from her partner, six months previously. They'd had a row, and she said that she would move out, and left the house. When she returned, "to make it up" she found all her things in dustbin sacks. She felt, "very hurt, gutted, powerless - want to turn the clocks back and can't, helpless, guilty, angry, alone, unsupported, and (of course, again) rejected". She intervened in several ways, and left herself "Better, laughing. I'm telling her she's too good for him!"

Now you can see the long reach of the statement that the unconscious mind is stacked associatively. Jane's feelings of rejection had a little to do with the incident six months ago, but were so much more strongly associated with those of the twelve and fourteen year old. Of course a mother does not reject a twelve-year-old by dying - but that's not the point. The youngster *felt* rejected. The sister didn't reject the younger one when fleeing from the wrath of her father, of course not, but the youngster felt "stranded". The feelings, which reached from the far past are now, mercifully, laid to rest.

You can deduce therefore, that a small incident as a child - say of a grazed knee, may be stored in the same 'file' or 'box' as a traumatic motor accident in which we were made to feel insignificant, and a shattered love affair, in which our feelings were denied. When the box or file is opened, not only will the feelings associated with the grazed knee emerge, but also the associated feelings from the other 'items' stored with it. Fortunately, however, most of the time these 'files' remain password protected. It's usually only when the whole storage system gets too full and overflows, that a little leakage occurs. This usually shows up as one of a whole range of symptoms and we have a clear message that something is wrong. If the illness or sense of 'wrong' persists, we usually do something about it by seeking help from the professional we believe will be able to solve the problem for us.

Price to Pay

Clearly our storage system is necessary for our health and survival in the world, and we invest a great deal of energy in making sure it's functioning efficiently. Even a perfectly functioning storage system exacts a price. The more efficiently we lock our feelings away, the less in touch we become with the way we feel, and also the more difficult it becomes to connect with others and to relate to what is going on around us.

Another thing happens when we deny a significant portion of the way we feel. In the first place, we start to believe that we must be totally insignificant and unimportant because there is no-one 'out there' able to validate us. Secondly, we assume that as 'out there' is right, and as it does not agree with our experience 'in here', *we* must be wrong. By logical deduction our perception and/or information processing system must be faulty. This means that we are unreliable, and unreliable, as we know, means 'no-good'. We no longer feel good about ourselves, or trust ourselves.   We grow suspicious, and we stop loving or even liking ourselves much at all.

Moment of Choice

If we react to situations because of all this stuff stored inside of us, surely it's not 'our fault' and there is nothing we can do to make things different?   Surely, by our own definition change isn't possible, ever? Surely things will just get worse and worse? Unlikely as it may seem at our deepest and darkest moment, it is possible to change the way we react. There is a process whereby we can turn 'react' into 'respond'.   This change is one of the first and most fundamental steps to achieving true **Peace of Mind.**

Let us explore this idea in a little more detail.   First we need to understand and accept that there is a perfectly good reason for the way we behave.   The reason may be well hidden, but it is there.   Where there is a reason, there is something to change, and where there is the possibility of change, there is a choice.   More than that, simply by becoming aware of the fact that we are 'reacting', that something is happening inside us to 'make' us act in a particular way, we start to become aware of how this feels.   We become aware of the 'build-up', of the way tension or emotion is welling up inside of us, and we become aware of the 'flash-point', where it quite literally explodes, and we are propelled forward into whatever action we take.   By being aware that there are stages to our process, we also realise that there is a moment before the 'flash-point'.   Leading up to this 'flash point', we can recognise the communication we have with ourselves.   We can become aware of the words and sentences we use in talking to ourselves.   Often these sentences go on in our heads constantly.

Albert Ellis, a famous psychiatrist, says that we must do two things here - first recognise the sentences, and recognise that our internalised construction of these sentences *creates* the problem, the bad feeling. Throughout his writing, he quite often paraphrases William Shakespeare, *"There's nothing in life but thinking makes it so".*

At this point, then we need to say, "Okay, if I created this bad feeling, I can also decide to do something about it". Ellis also says, rather comfortingly, that if we work half as hard at getting better as we did in making ourselves ill in the first place, we will actually get better very quickly.   So there are a few indicators to help us recognise the way in which we contribute to the way we react to situations - ways we can identify and change to 'flash point'. We can pay attention to *how it feels, and* we can pay attention to *what we say to ourselves.* By observing closely, we find that we can begin to pinpoint a very precise moment.

This can become for us a moment of choice. We can in this moment, if we choose, deflect the surge of our eruption into some other activity. There is a split second in time when we can change our automatic response. There is a moment just before anger, when we make the decision to be angry. There is a moment just before we lash out, when we can choose to change our reaction - if that's what we want. The simple act of becoming aware of the process within us brings us to the verge of being able to make a change. Think back to Exercise 1 a page or two ago. Think about acknowledging yourself and consider doing so. Give it a go! So many learned people in the world of counselling use the phrase "Acknowledgement is often enough!" That doesn't mean that it is always everything to everybody, but it IS often enough.

Decision for change

Decide to become more aware. Do your best to find that moment of choice just before an uncontrollable reaction. Sometimes this will be easy, such as when the situation is complex and needs a bit of thought. Other reactions are almost instantaneous. We can understand these instantaneous reactions if we think of secretarial shorthand. Symbols are used to express many words. In the same way a situation can 'squash up' the sentences we repeat to ourselves. This 'squashing up' has the effect of intensifying the associated emotions, and the eruption is immediate, rather than built up over time. If we could slow the process down, we would find that the things we say to ourselves are still there, and so too are the ways this makes us feel - hence the powerful reactions we sometimes have. By teasing apart and slowing down the events leading up to the reaction, we will see that even this "uncontrollable" reaction is, actually still under our control. Anger is a good example of a situation where the moment of choice is difficult to recognise. After all, if someone makes us angry, we get angry - there is little choice! It may become a little easier if we consider the distinction between someone *making* us angry, and *getting* angry as a result of something someone does. The difference is more than semantic - it relates to control and responsibility. We may think that something or someone makes us angry, but the reality is that we make ourselves angry by our perception of what is happening - and here, at this point, we most certainly do have a choice. We can choose (once we have learnt) how to respond to situations, and in this way we can accept the responsibility for ourselves, thereby regaining control.

EXERCISE 2

WHAT, EXACTLY, DO WE SAY TO MAKE OURSELVES FEEL BAD?
(Allow 10 minutes for this exercise)

Dr. Albert Ellis maintains that we cause our own discomfort by the way we process things in our own minds. He says that we "construct" the world by the sentences that we repeat to ourselves in our minds. The logical follow on from this is that if we do cause the problem, we too can alter it. WHAT exactly, were you saying to yourself just BEFORE you felt bad last time, or should I say, just before you made yourself feel bad?

1. Start to think of the words you use inside your head. This will be a set of sentences packed fairly tightly together. When you have isolated your sentences, start to write them out.

2. Some of the sentences will be reasonable and logical enough. Others, though, will be emotion-laden e.g.-

> "I can't stand this"
> "This is awful"
> "It makes me feel terrible when I …."

Keep the logical sentences. Challenge yourself with your use of the other ones. You need to convince yourself of the illogical nature of what you are saying, and keep gently challenging yourself. We say, "I can't stand it ", when this is a nonsensical phrase. The "it" in, "I can't stand it" implies that "it" has landed upon us from another planet or somewhere, and does not acknowledge the fact that we have personal control over our feelings. Of course you can stand the feeling you have given yourself. In reality you've probably done so many times before without the situation finishing you off. Having said this, acknowledging your feeling of discomfort is perfectly acceptable and in itself brings a sense of relief.

If the bad feeling you have given yourself appears to have come from someone else's action or what they have said to you, think for a minute. What did the other person intend? Did they intend to hurt you very much? I would put it to you that it is YOUR perception of what YOU think that THEY think about you that is causing the discomfort. Remember the old saying, "Sticks and stones will break your bones but words can never hurt you".

Challenge yourself and your reactions. Are **you** hurting **yourself** by what your

---

perceived view is of what you think that person thinks of you? God forbid that that person DID intend the hurt, but if they did intend to hurt you then you need to look at this relationship very closely. It is then up to you what you do about it. At least this perception offers you direct choices.

3. The most important thing to remember is to be kind to yourself. Change can take a while.

This distinction is true of all emotions. There may be qualities in a person or some aspect of his or her behaviour that causes some reaction in us. It may be frustration at certain habits, envy of achievements, or whatever, but in each case the response or reaction is *ours*. If we can own it, we can choose whether or not to have it.

As we strive to become more aware of our reactions it is a good idea to remember:

- to be kind to ourselves
- not to judge the way we feel, merely to observe it
- eliminate the words 'should' and 'should not' from our vocabulary
- that there is no such thing as right or wrong when it comes to feelings.

Feelings just "are", AND THAT'S OKAY!

With practice, we can get really fluent at this technique, and it is life changing. It may be a good idea to keep a diary or journal, to record feelings, to note whether we 'own' our feelings or feel that someone else caused them. The most important thing to remember is to be kind to ourselves. Change can take a while.

2

Dealing with Feelings

It is important to acknowledge the feelings of those around us - those they express as well as those they try to hide.   Below, in Exercise three, are some ways of helping both others and ourselves with our feelings.... It is OK to skip to that now, if you wish.

The simple act of listening acknowledges the reality of the way someone feels, and sends out a message that says 'you're important'. Being listened to makes people feel the way we would like to feel ourselves. If it is important to acknowledge the feelings of the adults around us, the way we deal with the feelings of the children in our lives can have far reaching consequences, as we have already seen. A step-by-step guide to listening can be found in Part II.

In addition to the way we feel, other patterns of response we exhibit as adults were probably learned as children. For example, a dislike of insects probably came from the reaction of a parent or a significant other in our lives when we were young. We watched others react in a certain way, and because of our love and respect for that person, we 'believed' their reaction, and adopted it as our own. Some of these patterns were very subtle, while others may have been quite overt, and in the form of clear messages, as we discussed in the pervious section.

There are two things to be learned from this. In the first place, if we have children, or deal with children in any way, we can cultivate an awareness of the way they express their feelings. We can consciously 'allow' them to have their own feelings and not 'give' them ones that actually belong to us. It is equally important to do this in relation to the adults in our lives. It is very easy to get into negative patterns with those close to us, such as partners or parents, where we don't allow or acknowledge the way they feel, or want to impose our views or feelings onto them.

Secondly, by gaining the awareness that our original patterns of response were learned in the first place, we discover that we are able to change the ones we don't particularly like, and that we can keep the ones we do like. As we saw, and have hopefully been practising, it is possible to choose how, or in fact whether we express a particular emotion. There is also the choice of changing response patterns we do not like by our awareness that most of our patterns were learned in the first place, and can therefore be changed.

EXERCISE 3

MORE ABOUT FEELINGS
(Allow 20 minutes thinking and/or writing time for this exercise)

Most people have not had a model of how to encourage their children and others to be sensitive, caring people. There is still a widespread belief that if you relate in an accepting way to children about their feelings, they will turn out to be wimps and weak minded.

Think for a minute or two about the likely long-term effect of denying people's feelings, particularly when they are younger. What do you think could happen to the child or young person that has the existence of their feelings denied?

I suggest that if this happens over a protracted length of time: -

- The person will probably learn to hide their feelings.

- The person probably learns not to trust their feelings.

- Some people may eventually learn not to feel!

- We need to realise the importance of being accepting of other people's feelings

WHAT COULD BE DONE INSTEAD OF DENYING FEELINGS IN THE OTHER?

I offer you some examples: -

Statement - "I don't feel like work today"

All the counselling books you could ever read will tell you the same thing. JUST ACKNOWLEDGING THE PERSON'S COMMENT IS OFTEN ENOUGH.

Possible response: - "So you don't feel like work."

Can you think of other acknowledging responses to the above statement? Please write a couple below …

Statement - "Mr. Jones is really getting on my nerves today"

Possible response: - "Mr. Jones is really getting on your nerves?"

Can you think of other possible responses? If so, write them below …

Statement - "When I heard about that threat of redundancy, I was frightened for my job. I thought it would be me next".

Possible response: - "You were frightened about losing your job."

How else could you acknowledge?

We all need to be able to express our feelings. It therefore has to be okay for others to express their feelings too. It's good to help people to express their feelings to their colleagues, friends & members of their family. I would now like to introduce a set of criteria for expressing feelings:

Expressing our feelings is the other side of the coin from accepting others, and we DO need to accept the importance of accepting our children's, and other people's feelings around us.

1. Ask yourself the following question, and please write down the answers in three or four points: -

   "If we want other people to be accepting of our feelings, what do you think is important about how we express them?"

   (i)

   (ii)

(iii)

You should end up with something similar to this: -

- STATE CLEARLY what you feel, think or want

- OWN IT FOR YOURSELF

- CARE FOR THE OTHER as well as yourself

Please use these as guidelines in your self-expression from now on. Give it a whirl! You have nothing to lose!

Here are some expansions of each point:

STATE CLEARLY - are you being concise and specific and using language the other can understand or are you being vague and beating about the bush.

OWN IT FOR YOURSELF - using "I" instead of "ONE". Saying "I feel" rather than "you make me feel"

CARE FOR THE OTHER - recognise that other people, both adults and children, can feel hurt when we dump our feelings on them, blame them for our woes, call them names and shout unnecessarily at them. It is possible to express our feelings without doing any of these things. People can have common confusion between 'think' and 'feel' in considering the coming exercise. Often people say 'I feel' when they are really expressing an opinion and actually mean 'I think'. e.g. 'I feel it's important for you to do your share of the work round here'.

2.   Background points:

- We do not live in isolation - often what we may want for ourselves is dependent on the co-operation of work mates, partners, other family members and friends.

- To enlist people in helping us towards getting what we want, we need to tell them clearly what we need and how we feel.

   Unfortunately for many of us, we have been conditioned to keep our feelings and wishes to ourselves, perhaps because when we were younger, we got used to people not listening to us or taking us seriously. It could also have been out of concern that our work-mates, partners and families will not be able to cope with our feelings. We may even have had negative experiences of expressing our thoughts and feelings and getting a poor reaction from others.

- •   How we express ourselves is crucial if doing so is to benefit us without risk to our relationships and other people.

I next want to give you a chance to come up with one feeling you can go away and share or use, using the guidelines mentioned above:

1. Come up with an actual situation of something that happens at home or work and the feelings that go with it.

2. Think through how to express the feelings as discussed above. (It may be helpful to write it down here instead of just thinking about it).

3. Express the complete statement in front of a mirror, or to a friend to try it out.

4. Feedback to yourself, or listen to your friend's feedback, and find out whether your message comes across straight and is successful in satisfying the conditions.

5. Write the feeling down and take it with you to send at home or work!

Labels

It can be quite difficult to communicate how we feel to another person, partly because to communicate something, we need to know and to understand it ourselves first. Unless we have been working with our feelings, and have retrieved the locked away portion of ourselves from our storage system, it is unlikely that we will find this process easy. It is more common to see the way we feel in terms of the behaviour of another person than purely in relation to ourselves. So instead of realising that we dislike it when someone treats us harshly and without consideration, we may see them as rude and ill mannered. We label their behaviour, and quite often by extension, their person as well. So the person who treated us badly becomes a rude person. The child who dropped the glass is a clumsy child, and the shop assistant who made a mistake is stupid.

Labels can be both positive and negative. Someone can be good, or clever, or attractive, as well as stupid and lazy and ugly. Whether positive or negative, labels can function in ways that are more often destructive than affirmative.

EXERCISE 4

LABELS REMEMBERED
(This may take about 10 minutes)

1. Think about how it felt to be labelled critically by your parents and indeed by any other adult in your early life. Do you / did you label others?

2. Come up with a specific description of the actual behaviour behind the label that conveys:

a) what, exactly, were you doing to get that label?"

b) what, exactly, were the other people doing to get that label?

3. Think about the label, whether it is a so-called "bad" label, or a so-called "good" one.

4. Have you still got it?

5. Where does it come from now?

6. Do you still have to keep it? Remember the choice is yours. Many of us sometimes act in ways that create self-fulfilling prophecies that confirm that we "are" a particular, previously labelled behaviour, rather than that we actually deserve to keep it.

Please remember that you have a choice here, and think of challenging yourself and doing something else with whatever caused the label, like describing the behaviour, rather than you, the person.

Labels as expression of our own feelings

When someone does something that annoys or upsets us, we usually react by using a label. Clumsy, stupid, lazy, rude, arrogant - often these 'negative' labels express the way the behaviour of another person makes *us* feel. By using a label, we are able to distance ourselves from our feeling by dumping responsibility onto the other person. Instead of, *"You stupid, clumsy child!"* when our child spills fruit juice on the carpet, we could acknowledge and express the way their action makes us feel, along the lines of, *"I feel really annoyed when that happens, because juice stains, and besides I've told you a hundred times to finish your drink in the kitchen!"* If we do this we focus on the behaviour and not on the individual, in other words, *we* separate the do-er from the deed.

Labels as self-fulfilling prophecy

Probably the single most negative effect of using labels is that when someone hears something often enough, they begin to believe what they hear. This is particularly true if the person is a child. At certain stages of our lives, external messages have infinitely more power than internal ones, and labels can exert great power over our behaviour. We therefore become what our accusers say we are.

Did you have a label? Do you still display the characteristic that your original labeller gave you?

Working within the context of **Peace of Mind** seminars it is both astonishing and sad how often childhood labels live on in our adult lives. In one group someone had been "clumsy", and another still thought of herself as "Fat Pat". It is easy to imagine how these labels must have hurt the young people concerned, as well as the adults testifying to the long reach of the label. The fact was that the adults often still carried the effect of the label.

Labels as judgement

It seems logical that "negative" labels are "bad" and "positive" labels are 'good'. In reality this is not the case, for the simple reason that generally, labels refer to individuals. Therefore, when we say someone is 'good', or 'clever' or 'pretty', it is as much a judgement based on arbitrary external criteria as a 'negative' label. As we've seen, 'negative' labels originate from the feelings of the speaker. Similarly 'positive' labels come from external systems of evaluation such as general attitudes of society -

good children are quiet and respectful to adults, or from the projected needs of the speaker.

EXERCISE 5

WHOSE NEEDS? - AS CHILDREN …
(This should take about 15 minutes)

1. Remember something that you used to do that your parents didn't like or something they used to do that you didn't like.

2. Write down the example taking care to describe in simple words what was actually going on rather than use labels.

3. Think to yourself … What do you think you (or your parent) was trying to do by behaving that way?

4. What was it about the behaviour that led you (or your parent) to get upset about?

Another example from our **Peace of Mind** workshops was of a "good girl". The parent using the label had intended to reinforce the good behaviour of the youngster, but the woman relating the story to us was almost tearful, realising that she had almost put herself in a "jail" - hadn't done normal teenage things because "good girls" didn't do things like that. Whether we use labels to criticise or to praise, it implies judgement more of the individual than of their actions. The alternative strategy would once more be to focus on the behaviour:

> I think the way you knuckle down to your homework every day is wonderful, instead of "You're a good boy / girl".

> You managed to balance your bike on one wheel all the way up the road without falling once! Instead of "You're so clever!"

Again, this way of constructing sentences separates the do-er from the deed as was mentioned in **Labels as expression of our own feelings** above.

Self Esteem

There is one quality above all others that determines how individuals respond to the circumstances in their lives, and that quality is self-esteem. Self esteem is how a person feels about him - or herself - whether they think they are OK as people, and the extent to which they feel they deserve the good things in life. Dorothy Corkille-Briggs (1975) describes self-esteem very accurately:

"High self-esteem is not a noisy conceit. It is a quiet sense of self-respect, a feeling of self worth. When you have it deep inside, you're glad you're you. Conceit is but a whitewash to cover low self-esteem. With high self-esteem, you don't waste time and energy in impressing others. You already know you have value ... feelings of self worth from the core of (the) personality can determine the use (made) of.... aptitudes and abilities. In fact, self-esteem is the mainspring that marks every (person) for success or failure as a human being".

It is extremely difficult to function effectively with a low level of personal worth or esteem. It affects how we see ourselves in relation to others, and therefore how we operate as a husband or wife, employer or employee, parent, friend, or in any other role we fulfil on a daily basis. Our basic self-esteem is usually established in childhood, and often remains that way, simply because we tend to place ourselves in situations that reinforce the way we see ourselves. Changing our level of self-esteem requires that we take certain actions that may be different to the way we normally behave.

Feeling Better

Consider giving yourself these gifts for a few weeks, and see how that makes you feel.

Be kind to yourself

This can take many forms. Basically it involves allowing yourself the latitude to make mistakes, or taking time out from your routine or responsibilities, or doing for yourself any of the many little things you find so easy to do for those you love. Eric Berne spoke of this in terms of 'strokes'. A stroke is a unit of attention, and can be positive or negative. A positive stroke is an expression of approval, such as a smile, a kind word, or a loving touch, while a negative stroke is the opposite - an expression of disapproval - an angry frown, a sharp word, or physical violence. Everyone needs strokes of one kind or another, and negative strokes are better than no strokes at all. Often as adults, our task is to stroke others, and we use so much energy doing this that we pay no attention to our own needs. We need strokes as much as anyone else does. There are two ways we can get the strokes we need - by giving them to ourselves and by getting them from others.

Stroking Ourselves

This simply means allowing ourselves the things we like in life, giving ourselves the treats that make us feel special, wearing the clothes that make us feel good, and generally allowing ourselves the time and space we deserve.

Getting Strokes from Others

This depends very much on effective communication. We often assume that people can read our minds, and know what we want and what we like without being told. Getting strokes from others depends on how good we are at letting them know what we want.

EXERCISE 6

LOOKING AFTER OURSELVES
(This exercise should take about 20 minutes)

Write down the answer to the following questions: -

1. What do you like doing just for you?

2. When did you last do it?

3. Could you do it more often?

4. What else could you do for yourself?

Love yourself

Strange as this may seem, it is asking rather a lot to expect another person to love us if we don't consider ourselves good enough for our own love. Or perhaps we find it difficult to love ourselves because that would be conceit. If we look back to where our resistance to this idea originates, we will come to understand a great deal about the way we approach life. Louise Hay (1991) identifies some of the ways in which we sabotage ourselves by acting or thinking negatively.

Self-criticism

It is an almost universal tendency to criticise and berate ourselves for not being as good as we feel we should be at a particular thing or activity. In fact 'should' is one of the most common words we apply to ourselves. We 'should' be better parents, better employees, and better people in general. Referring back to exercise 7, if we were asked to think of a list of things we were bad at, the chances are we would think of a lot pretty quickly!

EXERCISE 7

IN VALIDATION
(This may take about 10 minutes)

Think of the things you appreciate in yourself at work, or at home, or qualities that you have that you feel good about. It can be something quite simple. Write a list about how you are / what you do that you appreciate and like about yourself.

If you want, do this exercise with someone else and appreciate each other, giving your "partner" a verbal pat on the back, indeed, appreciate the person you have been listening to for their caring and competence. If necessary, help the other person to come up with things they feel good about, and if they get stuck in negative things, encourage them to move on.

MAKE SURE THAT YOU STICK WITH THE POSITIVE.

When asked to list everything we think we are good enough at, the chances are that after a great deal of thought we may come up with perhaps two or three items. If we then consider the number of things we do in the course of a day, we get a clear idea of the impossible standards we set ourselves as we try to evaluate 'well' in terms of our lives. Dr Winnicott, the eminent psychodynamic psychologist who specialised in working with children, wrote extensively on the nature and needs of children in a language that parents could understand, and introduced the concept of the 'GOOD-ENOUGH' parent. He made the point that in general, parents do the very best they know how at the time - and that given their circumstances, this is usually Good Enough.

When we do or complete any action, I am sure in my own mind that we are doing the best we can with what we are deciding at that moment, even if we decide a few minutes later, that we were mistaken!

EXERCISE 8

"GOOD ENOUGH"
(This can take as long as you wish. Please keep your list and add to it!)

Start your own list :-

- I am a good enough reader of this book (to help you start on your list)

- I am a good enough ....

- I am a good enough ....

- I am a good enough ....

- I am a good enough .... (etc.)

It is as well to complete this on a "good day" when you feel well resourced. Put you list where you can easily refer to it – the front of your diary, the kitchen wall or on your work desk.

John

I remember working with a General Practitioner who consulted me not feeling very good about himself or his life. He was the father of three small children and was living with them and his wife, the family being completed by a tortoiseshell cat. His wife had had an affair with his best friend, and the GP had completely taken this as if he was solely to blame, and not that there were three people in the scenario who all had their own reasons for behaving how they did. The man and wife parted company, and after due time I decided that he was perhaps less blameful and ready to start on his "Good enough" list. He was very fragile, and the task took him some time to complete, in terms of self-acceptance.

In the context of the above example, it is important for you to be patient with yourself as you make your list.   Writers such as Maria Montessori echo this idea, when talking about the behaviour of children. The judgement that a behaviour or action is NOT good enough comes from an externally applied value system.

I would urge the adoption of the philosophy of GOOD ENOUGH, to be applied liberally throughout our lives, both to ourselves and to others. It is possible to consider most behaviour as GOOD ENOUGH. It is not a matter of lowering standards, it is a matter of accepting and living in the present, the now.

If we drive a car, our driving skills may not win us a world championship title in racing or rally driving, but we are probably able to get from point A to point B safely - and thus for our needs, we may be GOOD ENOUGH as drivers. We may not be good cooks, or homemakers, but if we are reading this, we have probably not starved to death, and are therefore GOOD ENOUGH providers of food for our needs.   This reasoning can be extended to cover many of the activities we engage in on a daily basis, and by doing this, it can feel that the weight of the world is suddenly lifted from our shoulders. This is true in quite a literal sense, because when we consider ourselves GOOD ENOUGH, we take the bite out of the judgements the world passes on us daily - or at least the judgements we think the world is passing on us daily. When we think in terms of GOOD ENOUGH, suddenly our list of skills can grow quite considerably.

Even if we do not consider ourselves very good at a particular activity, by evaluating it honestly in terms of our needs and of the situation, we will find that often we judge ourselves (and others) by external standards that cannot be applied to all situations. Perhaps we are trying to cook like Aunt Sally, and until we can, we do not consider ourselves good enough. But if we add to the equation that Aunt Sally loved working in the kitchen, and in fact had the time to spend all day working at exotic culinary creations, and that we hold a regular job in addition to being chairperson of the local *Whatever Society*, suddenly we can see that our freezer-to-oven hotpot is in fact quite GOOD ENOUGH!

If we do not particularly want or need to do a certain thing, our 'failure' to 'achieve' in that area becomes a choice, and not a failure. There is therefore no point wasting time thinking critical thoughts about ourselves. The destructive habit of self-criticism is usually internalised at an early age, and is seldom updated to reflect an attitude consistent with our adult lifestyles. The idea of free choice and the Moment of Choice is one to remember. We internalised many of the ideas we have about ourselves at a time when it was necessary for our survival. Doing so was GOOD ENOUGH for that time. This is a different time, and we can change our attitudes accordingly. We can once again do the best that we know how at this time. We can begin to be gentle with ourselves. We can stop judging ourselves by the standards of others. Please go back to exercise 8 now and see if you can expand your list.

Remember also that the standard set by yourself as being GOOD ENOUGH can vary to cover different periods of your life. This can be enormously releasing.   As we get older, we have not got our earlier physical prowess. A mother who provides regular meals for her growing family may opt not to do that to the same extent forever. A wage earner may not always have to / want to or need to earn at the same rate forever. It is really OK for the GOOD ENOUGH levels to be regularly fluctuating.
The opposite of criticism is praise. To counteract the effects of self-criticism we can work on praising ourselves - when we do something 'good enough', we can allow ourselves to experience a sense of satisfaction, and we can praise ourselves. Another pleasant thing to do is to accept the compliments given by others without a 'yes but' response. We may be surprised at how often people express their appreciation of us - appreciation that we often disallow due to a false sense of humility.

Fear

One of the most unkind things we do to ourselves is to waste vast amounts of both time and energy worrying about things that will probably never happen, and half scaring ourselves to death in the process. Our bodies react physically to fear by producing an extra burst of energy. This is very useful when the fear is real, and we need to do something to get away from it. But when the fear is in our minds, the physical rush of adrenaline is not useful at all - in fact it produces the symptoms we know as stress. This process of turning molehills into mountains occurs for many reasons, almost all of them associated with the way we feel about ourselves. "What if ... I can't do the job...? Nobody likes me ... I forget what I wanted to say when I stand up in front of all those people ... they laugh at me ... I fail the test ... I fall on my face..."

The possibilities are endless, and share one thing in common. None of them have happened yet! Andrew Matthews, in his delightfully humorous book "Being Happy" (1988, p 38) has a simple solution to this problem.

"All you have is now. The measure of our peace of mind and the measure of our personal effectiveness are determined by how much we are able to live in the present moment. Regardless of what happened yesterday and what might happen tomorrow, NOW is where you are. From this point of view, the key to happiness and contentment must be in focusing our minds on the present moment".

Just think about it. How is the "now" in which you are reading this page? Is it all right? Maybe? Give or take a bit? Think about it. Any moments past have gone. Worrying about them will not help. When the next moment comes, and the next, it will be "now". Wasn't your "now" when I asked you - "are you really all right?" - really OK?

Impatience

We often expect a great deal more of ourselves than we would expect of anyone else. Whether it is about the time we allow ourselves to master a new skill, or the way we are unable to say 'no' to the demands of others, and overload ourselves with commitments, or simply the way we refuse to allow ourselves to make mistakes, we often have unrealistically high expectations of ourselves. Even the term 'mistake' implies a judgement. A wise teacher once said that there are no mistakes, only experiences.   This is restated in NLP terms (Neuro Linguistic Programming, which we will consider later) as, "There is no such thing as failure, only feedback". Whether we call it experience or feedback, it is a powerful idea, because it implies that we have choice, decision, and then experience, and whatever the outcome of the experience, it teaches us something, even if we learn that we do not want to repeat that experience. The power of this philosophy is that it prevents us from judging ourselves harshly, and allows us to learn from the experiences that we would previously have called mistakes.

Negative Thinking

There is a growing acceptance of the idea that thoughts exert a powerful influence on us and on our lives. Andrew Matthews (1988 p 57) explains how this works:

"...your mind works on pictures. When you say to yourself, 'I don't want to forget my book' you get a picture in your mind of forgetting. Although you say 'I don't want that', your mind still works on the picture and the result ... you forget your book. When you tell yourself 'I want to remember my book' you will have a mental picture of yourself remembering, and you will be in a far better position to remember. Your mind simply does not, cannot and will not work on the reverse of an idea."

The implications of this are enormous! Not only is it wise to think in positive terms about daily things we want to do or to experience in our lives, it also illustrates the self-fulfilling nature of our negative thoughts about ourselves. Because the mind takes things literally, we tend to set up life experiences which are in accord with the way we think - we surround ourselves with people who treat us in the way our mind tells us we should be treated, and this further reinforces and strengthens our pattern of belief. The belief becomes habitual, until 'that' (whatever the original negative thought told us) is the unchangeable 'way we are'. The solution to this is deceptively simple. First we need to become aware of our thoughts, then we can begin to change them, knowing of course that it is well within our power to change a thought. First there must be the awareness of the thought, then the awareness of the element of choice, then the choice to change. Thinking positive thoughts about ourselves leads to a positive belief system about life and ourselves in general, and can be the most empowering gift we give ourselves.

Techniques such as meditation and visualisation are valuable aids in the process of 'changing the mind', and are discussed in greater detail in Part II.

Comparisons

In our competitive world, where achievement is prized as that which gives the 'edge' or advantage over another person - our opponent, comparisons are necessary. We play along in this game by constantly comparing ourselves with other people. We invariably don't quite make the grade, because we will always find people who are 'better' than we are. Comparing ourselves with others is therefore one of the surest ways to conclude that we are wanting, thereby reinforcing our poor sense of worth. No matter how good we are at something in particular, there will always be someone, somewhere who is 'better' than us, and no matter how awful we consider ourselves to be in any area, there will always be someone who is 'worse' than us. It therefore makes no sense to compare ourselves to anyone else. What we should be doing is recognising our unique individuality and that we are the particular way we are for a very good reason (and incidentally, that which we are is as good as we can be at the present time - we are Good Enough).

This is not to say that we should be complacent, or that we should give ourselves an excuse to be lazy. We can always consider the way we used to be, and this will show us the extent to which we have grown and changed. If we find ourselves unable to resist the temptation to compare, we could attempt to confine ourselves to PBs or Personal Bests by looking at our achievements in the light of the way we used to be.

Lack of Support

Sometimes we seem to find ourselves totally alone in the world, and unable to cope with our lives. For most people the reality is more likely to be that our solitude is a result of choice - our choice not to allow others to assist us. We do this in many ways. Perhaps we pride ourselves on being self-reliant, so we never express a need for help. This comes back to the point we discussed earlier, that we expect others somehow to read our minds, and automatically know what it is that we need - or that in fact we need anything at all.

Perhaps we honestly do not believe that we are important enough to warrant a fuss being made. We feel that we ought to be able to cope - a mother struggling to meet the needs of her family and as well as fulfilling her obligations to her job; a husband struggling to fulfil the expectation that he earn enough to support a growing family on his own - the examples are endless. We do not live in isolation, and while it is often easy to reach out and help others, it can be difficult to allow others to do the same for us.

A common area that we express this inability to accept support from ourselves and from others is in the way we treat our physical bodies. We often drive ourselves to illness, and then still keep on going, insisting that we are 'okay', when we are clearly not! Some of us play the game the other way. Unable to cope, we express constant neediness, and demand support from others to such an extent that they withdraw, frightened by the force of our need. We are left without support, and the message we set ourselves up to receive is the same. We do not get support because we don't deserve it!

The way to break this cycle is once again to cultivate an awareness of the way we act and interact, and as we become aware of our patterns of behaviour, we gain the power to change.

The common theme running through all these examples is clear. We invest a great deal of energy in maintaining the image we have of ourselves, even if this involves deeply destructive cycles. Our belief in our worthlessness sets up a pattern of reinforcing events, and we find ourselves in situations with predictable outcomes. The key to changing this process is awareness, and ultimately, choice. Change is seldom comfortable, but one thing that it does for us, is that it builds awareness - and we find that we have initiated another cycle - this time a positive cycle. All we need to remember is that ultimately we *do* have the choice, and, that no matter how hopeless things appear, there is a moment - perhaps only a split second when we can choose to change things, this time.

Autobiography in Five Chapters by Portia Nelson

One   As I walk down the street,
        There is a deep hole in the sidewalk.
        I fall in.
        I am lost ... I am hopeless.
        It isn't my fault. It takes forever to find a way out.

Two   I walk down the same street.
        There is a deep hole in the sidewalk.
        I pretend I don't see it.
        I fall in again.
        I can't believe I'm in the same place.
        But it isn't my fault.
        It still takes a long time to get out.

Three   I walk down the same street.
        There is a deep hole in the sidewalk.
        I see it is there.
        I still fall in ... it's a habit.
        My eyes are open.
        I know where I am.
        It is my fault.
        I get out immediately.

Four   I walk down the same street.
        There is a deep hole in the sidewalk.
        I walk around it.

Five   I walk down another street ....

BUILDING BRIDGES

- Look after yourself. Start making little changes in your life that will get you even a tiny bit more of what you want - no need to go all out for change immediately - step by step will do.

- Practise sharing your feelings and also helping your partner, children, friends and colleagues to share their feelings.

3

The Child Within

We are a composite of all the things that have ever happened to us. This is obvious in some situations, as we have already discussed, such as in the way our reactions to situations often reflect or echo reactions to events from earlier stages of our lives. As we become aware of these reactions as patterns, we begin to realise just how much of our lives consist of similar patterns of behaviour. Research has shown that somewhere within us we carry the memory of absolutely everything that has ever happened to us. This means that we carry the memory of each event, *the way we experienced it at the time.* So unless we 'process' what happened in any given event, and by this we mean unless we take our experience of what happened, and change it by perhaps replaying it in our hearts and minds, or in some other way re-organising the way it caused us to feel or react, we store the memory of the event exactly as we understood it at the time, somewhere within ourselves.

So if we think back to our childhood now, we can ask *'Was it a happy childhood?' 'Did I feel loved and honoured and respected?'* If we can answer 'Yes' to these questions, we probably have a good chance of being able to live our lives in a creative and constructive way. If our early childhood contained these qualities, even if we are not happy at the moment, we probably possess the tools to change our circumstances in a way that brings us closer to what we want out of life. And if we did not have the benefit of this type of care and support in our childhood, we can call on our resources as adults to change the way our memories are stored, and go back and re-resource the small hurting child that we were.

Even in the happiest childhood, there were moments that weren't happy, and these too, are stored uncritically in our own personal storage system. As adults, our storage system is quite complex, and normally a great deal of processing takes place before events or experiences are laid down as memories. Take the following example:

The telephone rings at work, and it's your boss. Before you can say anything, s/he hurls insults at you, leaving you speechless by accusing you of something you didn't do, and threatens you with the loss of your job. You can't get a word in edgeways, and you have a less than clear idea about what the problem is. All you can follow is something about incomplete paperwork, and the consequence that month end figures are grossly distorted, reflecting badly on you, your department, and your very angry superior.

What happens inside when we are attacked like this? It is an awful experience, especially if we are unaware of any failure on our part. If our self-concept is bad to start off with, chances are, we will 'take on' a number of the insults aimed at us, and think in terms of what we did wrong, and what is going to happen to us as a consequence. We will internalise a significant portion of the tirade, because it will reinforce the way we experience ourselves anyway. As a good employee, we will probably make it our personal responsibility to correct the error, even if the fault turns out to lie far from our door.

A second possible response could be that we are so shocked by the event, that we immediately block significant portions of what transpired from our awareness. Later we may well remember that s/he said certain things to us, but we will no longer be at all upset, or perhaps we will even change our memory of the incident slightly, to reflect less blame on ourselves. We may still 'take on' many of the insults, and they will be stored as corroborating evidence of how useless we are anyway, or they may be totally hidden in our awareness, stored under 'those experiences that are so awful, I choose to forget them'.

Alternatively we may well and truly 'laugh it off', because we know deep down that none of the things said could possibly apply to us. Our response or reaction would be that our boss is having a bad time, and wants to know about something-or other to do with incorrect figures. In our storage system and memory, the event becomes 'the day the boss went ballistic about a mistake someone made.'

Yet another possibility is that we hear the insults and carefully consider them, matching them against the way we have come to know ourselves. We may choose to look critically at ourselves in case something in the way we project ourselves needs to be modified or altered.

As we can see, as adults we take our experiences and process them in some way *before* storing them as memories. Of course, our method of processing depends on the memories we have already laid down, and on the state of our self-concept, or how we feel about ourselves. As young children we didn't have the benefit of many memories, or even much of a constructed self-concept to guide us. Thus many of the memories we have are laid down much as we lived them at the time, without the benefit of processing them in any way.

If something rotten happened to us as a small child, like we fell and hurt ourselves, and we were feeling a little shaky to start off with, or the people around us were busy, and were unaware of our distress, the memory may be stored as 'nobody loves me.' Even if later our life experience proves to us that there are many people who care deeply about us, and we have subsequently come to know ourselves as a 'loved' person, that childhood memory is not taken out and re-classified as 'unfortunate accident'. It remains under 'I'm unloved'. Because the child sees itself as being at the centre of its own particular universe, it takes responsibility and guilt upon itself and the 'unlovedness', in its own mind, becomes 'unlovable'.

Part of the difficulty is that at the time of the incident, the feeling is too much for us to deal with, and therefore to protect us from ourselves, the unconscious mind shuts it down, and makes the emotion(s) related to the event "frozen in time". The feelings lie, dormant, and when a similar feeling or feelings arise at a later date (and remember, we have already said that the unconscious mind stores by association) then the feelings connected with the original events as well as the current ones can be activated.

How many times have we thought that either another or ourselves have over-reacted?

This is the reason for that process. Because the feelings from the earlier time were so raw, so un-processed, since we had not the ability to rationalise at the time of the incident, those same feelings spill out at the later date in their raw and often child-like strength. We may be convinced that this is the unconscious mind saying, "I'm now going to incapacitate you" – but in fact this is far from the case. The opposite is true. The unconscious mind is actually trying to help by allowing trapped feelings out!

It is therefore in quite a literal sense that we have within us the small child that we were, and as we journey towards full integration of ourselves, and set about optimising the way we live our lives, we need to pay some attention to this child within. Although we refer to stored memories when we speak of the child within, our memories are much more comprehensive than mere records on file. They include input from all our senses, and most certainly include the emotional content as well. So if we access a particular memory, we will recall not only the event as we experienced it, *but how we felt about it at the time*. We remember as the little child we were, and our adult response to this in the here and now must be to supply what the small child needed at the time if we want to re-process and re-classify the event.

This is why writers on this subject speak of the Child Within, and recommend that we treat that part of ourselves in the same way as we would treat a physically small child outside of ourselves. This may feel strange at first, especially to those of us who have learned to become terribly grown up about our lives. Remember that there is no need for anyone else to know what we are doing - that's the beauty of working with the child within - we can do it privately. But we do need to be aware that the strict or very mature adult we have become may well be that way (i.e.

very strict and mature) in order to control or suppress the huge pain which is threatening to overwhelm our child within.

By making our child happy, we release great amounts of the creative energy that was holding things together internally. Imagine being able to apply this energy to living our adult lives!

A great deal has been written about "The Child Within". Bruce Davis, in his book *"The Magical Child Within"* (1982) explains how the way we live our lives depends to a very large extent on the relationship we have with our child within. He bases some of his ideas on the theory of Transactional Analysis, and sees the child as that spontaneous part of us - the child we once were, but also the child that is very much alive and present in us each moment of each day.

How we relate or choose not to relate to this child determines to a very large extent not only how we live our lives, but also our quality of life. The only way we can ignore the child within is by running away - and in some cases this can be quite literal.

Davis explains how we are taught to ignore our child from quite an early stage of our lives, and how we become so 'busy' doing other things that the voice of our child is lost somewhere in the noise and confusion. We may engage in repetitive behaviours, such as overeating or smoking or drinking in an effort to still the muted cries of our child. Sometimes we live our entire lives in a way, which totally ignores our inner child. We may become very severe parent type people, who keep the child locked away in a high tower, like Rapunzel in the fairy tale, or we may drown the child in constant sensory input - whether it is work, drink, food or pleasure. There are many patterns of acting out, which deny the reality of the way we feel inside - the feelings of our inner child.

Davis' solution to this almost universal problem is that we allow ourselves a second childhood. He speaks not only of the process of growth from within, but discusses how this impacts on the external world, just as the presence of a small physical child affects others. Just as a physical child needs support from the environment, so our child needs an external world that is safe and supportive if it is to venture out. This can mean something as simple as setting aside time for yourself to do the things you need to do, without being imposed upon by the needs of others. Sometimes this is difficult - but even an hour or two in a 'safe' place will be Good Enough.

So, let us assume that we choose to begin looking at our lives in this perhaps unusual way and that we want to listen to that little voice and respond to the feeling inside. What can we do? How can we begin to free ourselves from the voices of others telling us what to do, or how to live our lives?

Self Acceptance

When we were children, and something went wrong, our natural response would have been to wonder what we had done wrong. This would have been true no matter what the situation. If our parents had a fight, we would have felt responsible. We may have felt that the fault was because of something we did, or perhaps even just because we were 'there'. If the event or events for which we felt responsible was traumatic enough - if it had serious consequences, it may have become necessary to 'punish' ourselves (subconsciously) in the hope that things would go back to the way they were before. At the very least we would have scolded ourselves for our bad behaviour, and this would have built into a pattern that we carried through to adulthood. As adults we continue to scold our child, and we can hear this if we listen to the number of times we send ourselves the negative messages that reinforce our poor sense of self - Ellis' sentences that we repeat to ourselves over and over. Responding to these negative messages is like responding to one of those radio signals scientists sent into space many years ago to make contact with intelligent life 'out there'. The source of the radio signals is no more 'alive' today than the messages we give ourselves. The signals relate to a different time and a different reality, and all that makes them relevant to the present time is the fact that it is our child within that is responding. If we use our adult creative intelligence to begin to see what we are doing and to understand the patterns of behaviour that hold us captive, we can accept those parts of ourselves that we previously rejected, and we can bring ourselves more into the present reality.

Communication

It seems both obvious and strange to suggest communicating with our inner child. One way of doing this is by becoming aware of the little voice within, but if we have been spending a great deal of time denying our child, this may be quite difficult to do.

Play is a powerful means of communicating with children, and we can apply it to our child as well. Expressive media such as art - drawing or painting, sewing, three dimensional collage work, and so on, are obvious choices, as is clay, sculpting or sand play. Playing with sand and in the sand does amazing things for children. It's no accident that some people have violent reactions to sand. Some people dislike sand because it's 'messy', while others don't like the texture. Gardening and digging in the dirt is also very therapeutic, as any gardener will tell you, although the more structured and goal oriented the activity, the less the child will be able to express it self spontaneously.

The inner child is very much associated with creativity, and has been related to the activity of the right half of the brain. It makes sense therefore to think that by accessing what is popularly called 'the right brain'; we are coming closer to communicating with our inner child.

EXERCISE 9

PLAY THERAPY
(Take as long as you wish over this)

Play is a powerful means of communicating with children, and we can apply it to the inner part of ourselves, our child part that lives inside us all as well. How about a project in an expressive medium? : -

An Art based one on paper:
- Drawing
- Painting
- Charcoal
- felt-tips
- pastels

Something which may take a little longer such as:
- sewing
- three dimensional collage work
- clay work at a pottery class

How about selecting an ongoing project? Spontaneous things can be very helpful:
- sand play (this does amazing things for children)
- digging in the dirt
- gardening and is also very therapeutic, as any gardener will tell you

Remember, the more structured and goal oriented the activity, the less the child part of you will be able to express itself spontaneously. A short dig in a heap of soil or sand would also be most acceptable.

Writing or drawing is one way of doing this. Louise Hay (1991) recommends using your non-dominant hand to draw a picture and Exercise 10, which follows, provides you with an opportunity to do this.

EXERCISE 10

DRAWING WITH YOUR INNER CHILD
(The time required for this may vary, 5 or 10 minutes is enough to make a start)

The inner child is very much associated with creativity, and has been related to the activity of the right half of the brain. It makes sense therefore to think that by accessing what is popularly called 'the right brain'; we are coming closer to communicating with our inner child.

Louise Hay recommends using your non-dominant hand to draw a picture.

If you allow yourself to do everything with your non-dominant hand, including the choice of colours, and just relax into the process, amazing insights can be achieved. Even more so if you can suspend judgement about the quality of the picture that emerges, remembering that it is a young child doing the drawing.

1. Sit with your unlined paper pad on your knee in front of you.

2. Hold your pen or pencil in your non-dominant hand.

3. Choose colours also with your non-dominant hand.

4. Relax.

5. Ask your inner child to draw a picture about a certain event in your life, and just allow it to happen. You could ask your child to draw a picture of you, or to represent your life path - the things that happened to you, or a picture of your family, or the significant people in your life.

6. Without looking at your paper, let your writing implement draw.

---

7.   How are you doing? Amazing insights can be achieved.

8.   So much the better if you can suspend judgement about the quality of the drawing, remembering that it the young child from inside you doing the drawing.

If a physical child presented you with the drawing that you see emerging from beneath your hand, you would accept it without judgement. You would appreciate the skill of the child, given its age, and may even experience a sense of love in your heart.

If you can have this sense of love for your inner child in your heart, the process of opening to yourself will proceed in leaps and bounds. It may feel strange, or even a bit silly, especially at first, so you will probably want to be quite private when you do this. (In reaching for your inner child, don't alienate your parent or adult - they are part of you too!)

Notice if you feel any differently, or whether the way you feel is perhaps coming from a slightly different place within you.

Another powerful technique that Louise Hay recommends is to use a photograph of yourself as a child to try to re-connect with the part of you captured frozen in time in the picture. Exercise 11 describes how to do this.

Altered Awareness

You can reach your inner child is by altering your awareness - accessing the memory as it is stored. This is a powerful and direct method, and in most cases is a journey we are advised to take only with the aid and support of someone professionally trained.

To explain why we say this, let us use an analogy that can be easily understood. We can compare our minds/brains to a very complex computer system. To run our computer selves properly, we employ a computer operator who is also a very skilled programmer. Over time this individual has worked out the programme that we know as ourselves – the personality we show to the world and the way we feel inside. Our programmer has been with us for a long time, and together we have figured out how this system works.

EXERCISE 11

LOOKING AT YOUR INNER CHILD
(10 minutes should be enough time to start this - though 20 minutes would be a more leisurely go at it)

1. Find a photograph of yourself as a child.

2. Look carefully at the photograph, and try to connect with what you see. If you have several photos of yourself as a child, better still. Try to connect with the part of you that was frozen in time in each photo.

3. Another very powerful way to do a similar thing is to seat yourself in front of a mirror, and look deeply into your own eyes, and find the child hidden in there.

4. Talk to yourself while you do this. Talking to your child, perhaps using something other than your present name, like a childhood nickname helps to initiate communication. Speak to your inner child as if it were a real child. It helps if you had a nickname as a child.

5. Note what it feels like when you use a name like this. For many of us there is some slight gut reaction, because a child nick-name is something that we "grew out of" and its use may well take us a little distance back to where we once were. This is good, because it means that we are a little closer to communicating with our inner child.

6. Whether or not there was a nick-name, begin talking to your inner child as if he or she is a physical child. Ask what the child would like to do, or what the child feels about any situation. A particularly nurturing thing to do is to take some time - say a weekend, or a day, or even a few hours when external demands can be ignored, or at least minimised, and prepare your house as if a child was coming. Take your child to the supermarket, and ask what type of food they would like in preparation for your 'special time' together. Or plan an outing – something the child would really like.

7. Again ask the child what they would like to do - and as the loving parent of the child, do all you can to make it possible. It may be something you've always wanted to do as a child, but were never allowed or able to do. Give yourself the treat.

Our programmer has sorted all our internal files in a way which only the two of us understand. The things we like are easily accessible while the things we don't like are put in a place that we seldom go, and there are files that are so secret that we've even forgotten about them, and there are files that need a special password to access. In all probability parts of our child are in these files. The important thing to know is that our programmer arranges things the way they are so that we can function in the best way possible.

What happens when we enter an altered state, is that this programmer is by-passed to some extent. If we reach an altered state via sleep, we could perhaps surmise that the programmer has left a junior person in charge, and some of the secret material gets out - but usually in coded form, and we experience it as dreams. If we reach an altered state via meditation, we enter this state with the consent of the programmer. We get to browse the files with the programmer watching carefully. It may happen that our programmer dozes off briefly, and we get a glimpse of something in a secret file, but always the programmer is there either to censor or edit the material quite quickly, or to integrate the information in a harmless or better still, a useful way. Still following this analogy, the process of learning to meditate can be compared to a process of gaining the trust of the programmer. Slowly, little by little, the programmer allows us deeper and deeper into the secret files, and helps us to integrate what we have learned from there.

Another way to reach and altered state, and thereby access our inner child, is via hypnosis. This is by far the quickest and most direct route. The skilled practitioner lulls the programmer to a state sometimes mis-labelled as sleep, and allows us to access the secret files without having to de-code them. What must be remembered about this state is that the programme still runs, so it is not as though there is instant access into every part of the system. The programme determines which files are nearest the surface, and which are more deeply hidden, and also which are filed together. If anything goes wrong, and alarms start going off, the programmer returns to his or her post, and access to the system is denied.

This analogy makes it clear that using altered state to access your inner child can be difficult or even traumatic, because a great deal of previously hidden information may surface, and if the programmer isn't there to help integrate it, damage to the system can occur. Search diligently for the hypnotherapist that makes both you and your child feel comfortable. When you find one, this method of working is greatly recommended, because you can make tremendous progress with the skilled help of another person. **Peace of Mind**™ has a partner, Mnemodynamics Unlimited, and the Mnemodynamic Register website has a list of therapists trained in its own method, Mnemodynamic Therapy.

Whichever way you make a connection with you inner child, give that child the most important message you can give any child. Let that child know that you love him or her, and that he or she is not alone. Wonderful and important as relationships are with other people in our lives, the one relationship that will always be with us is the relationship we have with ourselves. We will always be there, and as we work towards making that relationship a positive one, whereby we love and honour and approve of ourselves, we will find that our lives will assume a new dimension, and we will begin to have a sense of the sun coming through the clouds after a very long, dark winter.

4

Needs and Wants

Who are we?

Before we can express our needs, we must be aware of them ourselves, and tied up with this, is the issue of personal identity. The question 'Who am I?' is such a difficult one to answer that it has become subject of a philosophical debate which has occupied the greatest human minds throughout the ages. The need for a personal identity is however an immediate one, and one which we often resolve by identifying ourselves in relationship with others, or in terms of our function in the world. We are *a mother' 'a father' 'a lawyer' 'an accountant' 'John's wife' 'Sally's father'* and so on. Our identification with social or externally determined roles can be so profound that it can at times rob us of our very lives. The position of women in many societies is a good example of this. We need only to consider the extremes of physical or emotional mutilation, or even death, to which women have been subjected to appreciate the extent to which this is true. Historically, women in Western culture have identified themselves by their role as wife or mother, and all other concerns have been subservient to this function. Although it is fair to say that these stereotypes *are* changing, many of us, men and women alike, are still only able to define ourselves in relationship to the external world.

When we know ourselves only from the outside, it is difficult to know our needs, as they are experienced internally. When this happens, we place the needs of our role above our individual needs. This devalues us, and makes us feel that our needs 'don't matter'. As we grow within ourselves and come to realise that we are important and valuable people, it becomes easier to express our needs and to take the necessary steps to fill them. It is important that we learn to differentiate between those needs which are genuinely our own, and those needs we experience as a result of the influence exerted by the outside world.

Peer pressure is an example of a need forced from the outside. Needs of this type are obvious in children or young adults, when 'everyone else' has or does what we want. The desired object in this case is not the real focus of the need - the need is for peer approval and acceptance. The object is *wanted* to fulfil that need. It is easy to see the difference between a need and a want in a case such as this.

Behaviour is very much determined by both needs and wants, and many of the problems we experience in relationships come from the needs or wants of one impinging on the fulfilment of the needs or wants of another. This will be discussed more fully in the next section.

Hierarchy of Needs

The nature of human needs has been theorised upon by many, but perhaps the most well known classification of needs is the Hierarchy of Needs as defined by American psychologist Abraham Maslow. He placed human needs in a hierarchy not of importance, but of priority. Only when the needs on the lowest level have been fulfilled can we begin to put energy into getting 'higher level' needs fulfilled. For example, if we are hungry and have no food or way of obtaining food, we may enter a space of physical danger to fulfil our physical need. In so called 'primitive' societies hunting for food placed the hunter in physical danger (negating the level 2 need for safety and protection). In the same way a relationship (level 3 need) may be sacrificed to fulfil physical needs for food and shelter if the need arises.

Needs or Wants

Our society is characterised by a sort of 'more and more' syndrome. Some would say that it is not only our society, but the nature of the universe itself which is expanding, always getting bigger, and *more.* We always seem to want something, and when we get it we do not feel satisfied, so we focus our attention on wanting something else. The key to understanding this phenomenon lies therefore not in finding the object or outcome of our desires, but in investigating the process of our desiring.

According to Maslow, once we have achieved the fulfilment of the needs on one level of the hierarchy, we can begin on the second level. In practise there is a degree of flow between levels. We may find ourselves unemployed and in serious danger of not meeting our physical needs, while simultaneously being concerned with the level 4 needs of recognition, acceptance and a sense of competency.

There is also the possibility that although we are in possession of a healthy bank balance, and have totally fulfilled level 1 and 2 needs, that we continue to strive for greater success and financial security, even to the detriment of the higher level needs that Maslow suggests should now be enjoying our attention.

American analyst and writer of 'Primal Scream' and other groundbreaking works, Arthur Janov has an interesting explanation for this. He includes the need for love as a level 1 need, perhaps even more fundamental than the need for food and safety. As proof of this, he cites hundreds of examples of the way institutionalised infants fail to thrive when not handled and 'loved' by staff, in spite of having all their other needs fulfilled.

According to Janov's theory, when a need is not fulfilled in early life, the individual experiences what he calls Pain, with a capital P. There is a certain logic to this because the non-fulfilment of level 1 needs poses a survival threat to a young organism, which must result in considerable stress, and we know from numerous studies that stress has a profound and potentially fatal effect on the body. Janov goes on to suggest that this Pain is stored as a memory in a cumulative fashion. Each time a need is not met, Pain is the consequence, and is stored. There is only so much Pain an organism can process, and a point is reached when a 'split' occurs, and the individual is no longer aware of their needs in an immediate and organismic sense.   Henceforth Janov contends we respond only to *wants*, and these wants are subconsciously driven in the direction of fulfilling our originally unfulfilled needs. Because we are no longer responding to our original impulses but to a shadowy memory, we will never be satisfied, no matter 'how much' of the desired outcome or object we achieve.

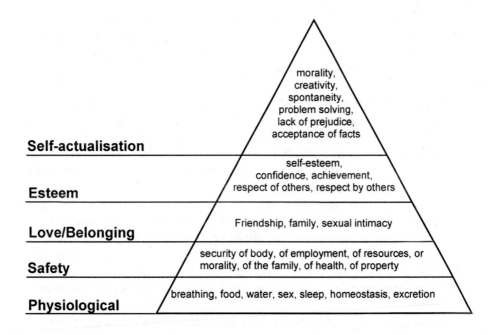

Diagram of Maslow's hierarchy of needs, represented as a pyramid with more primitive needs at the bottom

Janov says that this process of disconnectedness accounts for the obsessive nature of much of society, and the inability of many to reach a point of inner peace. The inability to satisfy Maslow's level 1 needs clearly makes it more difficult to move on to the fulfilment of higher order needs.

Although the specifics of this theory are not universally accepted, it does draw attention to the distinct differences between needs and wants.

According to Janov's theory, when a need is not fulfilled in early life, the individual experiences what he calls Pain, with a capital P. There is a certain logic to this because the non-fulfilment of level 1 needs poses a survival threat to a young organism, which must result in considerable stress, and we know from numerous studies that stress has a profound and potentially fatal effect on the body. Janov goes on to suggest that this Pain is stored as a memory in a cumulative fashion. Each time a need is not met, Pain is the consequence, and is stored. There is only so much Pain an organism can process, and a point is reached when a 'split' occurs, and the individual is no longer aware of their needs in an immediate and organismic sense.

Henceforth Janov contends we respond only to *wants*, and these wants are subconsciously driven in the direction of fulfilling our originally unfulfilled needs. Because we are no longer responding to our original impulses but to a shadowy memory, we will never be satisfied, no matter 'how much' of the desired outcome or object we achieve. According to him, this process of disconnectedness accounts for the obsessive nature of much of society, and the inability of many to reach a point of inner peace. The inability to satisfy Maslow's level 1 needs clearly makes it more difficult to move on to the fulfilment of higher order needs. Although the specifics of this theory are not universally accepted, it does draw attention to the distinct differences between needs and wants.

As with all our behaviour, the greater our awareness of the *why* behind our needs or wants, the greater the influence we can exert on our own destiny. It can be compared to shooting towards a target. If it is dark and we have only a general idea of where we should aim, we have very little chance of hitting the target. By understanding our motivations, we shed light on the outcome we desire, and we have a greater chance of aiming true.

What is the difference between a need and a want? A want is the way we have chosen, perhaps unconsciously, to satisfy a need.

Examples:
I need reliable transport; I want a new car or a yearly bus pass etc.
I need love; I want a monogamous relationship, or I want a baby etc.

EXERCISE 12

MEETING NEEDS
(Please do this by yourself for 15 minutes or so)

What do we mean by needs? A need = healthy condition for a healthy life.

1. Think to yourself, and write down the answer to the question:

    "What do I want?"

2. Then think, and write down the answer to the question:

    "What will that do for me?"

3. Work through this process until you get to what seems to you to be the

    "bottom line".

4. Look through the exercise

(Do the best you know how! I want you to be able to benefit from the answer).

I need to feel I belong and am part of the crowd; I want to dress fashionably, or
I want to join a group like a church, a sports group etc.

By posing the question "What will that do for you?" or "What will that satisfy?" we can get below the want level and begin to find the need level underneath.

Example: I need to get some qualifications.
              "What will that do for you?"
              It will mean I can get a job.

              "What will that do for you?"
              I will be able to earn and contribute to the family finances.

              "What will that do for you?"

I will feel more equal in my relationship with my partner.

"What will that do for you?"
I will feel powerful and a person in my own right.

This is a very useful process to go through. Having started with one solution, a quite different need has been uncovered at the bottom. There are MANY ways to satisfy that need. Even if the person concerned still goes on with their original plan, they are much more aware of why they want to do it. Sometimes, because of the choices open to us at the time, we may have chosen a way to satisfy is a need that could in fact be better met another way. Sometimes choices we made don't turn out the way we thought and hoped they would. Being aware of the need allows US to choose the most useful and fulfilling path.

It may be that you already get your own needs met. If so, WONDERFUL!

Why?

The little word 'Why?' is a very powerful one when it comes to establishing true motivation. The process of locking on to a specific objective or an objective to fulfil a need is primarily a subconscious one, involving sometimes convoluted paths of reasoning that take us far away from our true needs. In Janov's terms, we respond to wants rather than needs. Here is an example:

Jim

Jim had a job that required him to work a long day and spend many hours on the road. Although he received a reasonable salary at the end of the month, it wasn't enough to meet the needs of a wife and teenage family. He was competent at what he did, and was satisfied with the level of status within his company and among his peers. He believed he was happy in his job, in spite of the extraordinary long hours and high levels of stress.

In spite of a happy family life, he experienced a sense of discomfort, which he ascribed to his immediate financial difficulties, and each week he religiously bought a ticket for the lottery and fantasised about what he would do should he win 'the big one'. He dreamed of being able to support his family in the way he would like, and of giving up his job and opening a deep-sea scuba diving business in a seaside resort town. Week after week he bought a ticket and dreamed his dream.

One day a friend asked for help setting up a small business. He was glad to help, and spent the few spare hours he had planning and strategising with his friend. The business began to prosper, and the friend offered him a partnership. The business was still young, and joining his friend would necessitate a drop in income, and he was aware that there were no guarantees of ultimate success in a competitive market. After very careful consideration, he decided to join his friend.

That week when he bought his usual lottery ticket, Jim made a startling discovery. He became aware that he would not choose to change anything in his life if he won. The money he would get from a lottery win would be welcome, but it was no longer important - it was no longer a 'way out' for him.

Clearly Jim's 'need' to win the lottery was not based on his need for financial security. He spent many uncomfortable years believing that he needed money to change his sense of discomfort, so he worked harder and longer, and dreamed and schemed to find a way to increase his income. He was fortunate that his solution presented itself at his door, or he may have continued, like most of us, for the rest of his life looking for the miracle of chance that would be his salvation.

The Why Game

Consider any one of the things you want in your life. The need for more money is universal enough to use as an example. Let's consider Jim's desire to win the lottery. Assume you want to win the lottery and ask yourself:

'Why do I want to win the lottery?'
The answer may be 'Because I want to pay off all my debts.'

Ask again 'Why do I want to pay off my debts?'
Perhaps it's 'Because I feel uncomfortable owing money.'

'Why do I feel uncomfortable owing money?'
'Because then people think I'm unsuccessful / can't manage my affairs / am unable to earn enough ...etc.'

By following this line of questioning a completely different picture may emerge, and it may be possible to modify the behaviour you undertake to fulfil your needs. It is important to be honest with yourself. It is of course always possible to block yourself, or to reach a point where the only possible answer is 'because I want it!' Check whether this is because you have reached a real NEED (use Maslow's hierarchy as a guideline) or because you are feeling uncomfortable. If you can be open-minded and accepting of what you come up with, you may discover some interesting things about what motivates you.

EXERCISE 13

ACTION PLAN
(This should take about 15 minutes)

1. Work out for yourself what you have learnt from Exercise 12 and what you have written. Examples of the sort of questions you can ask yourself are:

    - Do you notice any patterns? Any surprises?
    - How many times do you say "often"?
    - How many times do you say "rarely"?
    - How would you have liked your answers to have been different?

2. Go through the first two items that you marked as sometimes or less frequent and ask yourself the question: "What will that do for you?" Stick with each item until you reach the bottom line and then brainstorm other ways to satisfy that same need.

3. With any time left, you could work with a friend or partner to help each other brainstorm ways to find some more ways to nurture ourselves.

4. Make a commitment to yourself, and each other if you worked that way, to make some changes.

Our needs are important

It is clear that if we place little value on ourselves as human beings, we will also place little value on our needs. We will tend always to place the needs and wants of others before our own. As we have already seen, many of our patterns of behaviour originate in childhood, in response to the impact we observe ourselves as having on our environment. If as children, our needs were always ignored, the result will be that we do not value ourselves in general terms, but more specifically, that we do not value our needs. Then, when we experience a need, and someone else comes along with a conflicting need, we will almost invariably step down, because after all, their need is more important. It is very easy to justify this behaviour in our society as unselfish, or as virtuous 'selflessness', which is not quite the same as being able to compromise.

Very few are able, or wish to live in such isolation that none of their needs will conflict with the needs of others. On the contrary, the fulfilment of many of our needs requires the presence of other human beings. This makes the need fulfilment a tricky social issue. By applying certain ground rules it is possible to overcome all obstacles.

The first thing to consider is the distinction between needs and wants. The closer we come to establishing our real needs, the less energy we waste on chasing phantoms, and the more we can focus on positive strategies.

Secondly, if we recognise that our needs are as important as the needs of others, and that the converse is true as well - in other words that the needs of everyone are 100% important, we can create a climate of mutual respect and foster a sense of co-operation. Whether our pattern of behaviour places the needs of others above our own, or whether we ram-rail our needs through in an attitude of survival of the fittest, we devalue ourselves and others and our pattern pushes being in a state of **Peace of Mind** further and further away. In fact, if we were to apply the 'Why push Game' to either of these behaviours we will come up with interesting points about the way we relate to the world, and about what our true needs are.

Need-fulfilment Strategies

We learn behaviour strategies at a very early age. We soon discover that if we act in a particular way we get what we want, and if we act in another way, we don't. This depends on the significant adults in our lives when we are young. The reaction of these people tends to be quite consistent towards us, even if this means that they are consistently inconsistent. This sets up a pattern of response in us, which remains fixed unless we experience overwhelming responses that make us change, or we become aware of our patterns. Although there is literally an infinite number of ways in which we act to fulfil our needs, we can distil these down to three broad categories, namely *submissive* behaviour, *aggressive* behaviour and *assertive* behaviour. It is important to remember that these exist along a continuum, and that we sometimes use different types of response with different people or situations. Although our behaviour may lean more or less strongly towards one of these broad categories, we will present examples of only the 'typical' or 'average' response. Again, most of these behaviours are simply behaviours that we have 'learned' at one stage or other of our lives, and by becoming aware of them we gain the power to change them.

Behaviour Patterns

Submissive

Submissive body language is very distinctive, and in an habitually submissive person can usually be identified by posture and head position. If we look at submissive animal behaviour it's easy to see where these physical patterns come from. An animal bows to the superiority of another by exposing itself as weak. The most visible sign of this is often an exposed belly, the most vulnerable part of the body. Lowered eyes and avoidance of eye contact is another clear sign, as is a general slinking, tail between-the legs gait. The submissive human is also bowing to the 'superiority' of another, and exhibits similar visible signs. There is an avoidance of eye contact, and a hunched posture, probably in an effort to be lower than the other as a parallel to the animal lying on the ground, belly up. It is interesting to watch this behaviour in others or ourselves in this context and to realise where and when we engage in it. We may act this way in response to a specific person, such as a parent figure or a boss, while at other times we walk tall, and respond in more assertive ways.

Sometimes the messages of our inadequacies are so pervasive that we become habitually submissive. We adopt a hunched posture, and find eye contact difficult. We feel uncomfortable in the presence of others, and fidget and shuffle and mumble. But even in this 'lowered' state, we have needs - in fact our needs are probably more extensive and greater than the needs of others. So, with the pragmatism and resilience characteristic of the human spirit, we may learn to adapt our submissive behaviour to get others to fulfil our needs. In time this pattern becomes comfortable and normal for us, and we manage to get by. We enjoy the fact that we never have to take responsibility for anything, because after all, we are inherently weak. This weakness compels others to 'help' and 'protect' us, and takes away the need to be anything but 'weak'.

Manipulation by guilt is one of the tools often employed by habitually submissive people, and this immediately brings to mind the elderly relative, confined to bed with some infirmity, real or imagined, who has hoards of people jumping to their every whimper. Taken to this extreme, it is unlikely that this represents truly submissive behaviour. It is more likely that the originally submissive person has discovered the tools for aggressive domination, and is applying them with relish.

Attractive though this model may be to those needing to exert power and control over others, there is a significant down side. The submissive person is totally dependent on others for the fulfilment of their needs. This means that their needs will frequently be subservient to the needs of the 'other'. This can result in a 'martyr' complex, with consequent rejection and resentment by the original carer. Someone is usually habitually subservient because of a basic sense of unworthiness, and negative responses from others such as resentment or rejection will only make matters worse. It can get so bad that the individual looses all sense of self, and may even loose total contact with what they need to ensure their physical survival.

Aggressive

It is an interesting paradox that the underlying motivators of aggressive behaviour are the same as that of submissive behaviour. Somewhere along the line habitually aggressive individuals have just learned different responses to similar feelings. Aggressive people feel as threatened and worthless as submissive people. The only difference is that they have not lost their natural ability to fight to assert their supremacy. Using the model we presented earlier, we can surmise that their aggression stems from a need to survive, and in their view of the world, the 'want' is for domination. Aggression is a learned strategy for achieving this. The aggressive attitude and behaviour continues no matter how often it is successful and the want is fulfilled. This is precisely because it is a want, or displaced need and not a true need in the sense of Maslow's hierarchy of needs.

The body language and attitude of habitually aggressive people suggests domination, and includes features such as arrogance, sarcasm, a strutting posture and a challenging glare. They often point fingers, make fists, or display physical aggression.

On the plus side, habitually aggressive people often get what they want by virtue of 'shouting the loudest', and can find it easy to achieve success and the accumulation of material possessions. Sadly this is often achieved at the expense of others. On the down side, the empires they build tend to be brittle, and collapse easily.   They struggle to fulfil emotional or relationship needs, and the need for esteem from both self and others remains elusively out of range.   Habitually aggressive people build themselves into ivory towers by unconsciously repeating the behaviour that builds the isolating walls higher and higher.

Assertive

The third category of behaviour is based on an open and honest communication with self and with the environment.   Assertive behaviour stems from an attitude to life, which is characterised by a sense of ease and flow, and an ability to vary responses appropriately to differing situations and to adapt to circumstances with a type of intelligent fluidity.

Assertive behaviour will appear in the presence of self-respect and respect for others.   If we are able to value ourselves and our needs, as well as others and their needs as 100% important, without elevating one over another, we begin to approach assertiveness.   An assertive individual is one who is able to compromise, and to balance his or her own needs responsibly with the needs of others, without acting in a way that is disadvantageous to anyone.   True assertiveness is the only way to peaceful coexistence.   It is also the only way to a sense of inner peace, and therefore true peace of mind.

Problem Ownership

A reality of life is that no matter how appropriate and assertive our need-filling behaviour, occasions will arise when our needs or the needs of others are thwarted.   These are challenging situations, and the strategies we need to adopt to solve them can require our best creative efforts.   Others will not always share our sense of fairness and our open-mindedness.   We may need to resolve our differences with people whose patterns of behaviour are less flexible than our own.   It is these situations that both challenge us, and teach us the most, and are also a measure of our progress towards an inner state of peace.   In the words of Martin Luther King: *'The ultimate measure of a man is not where he stands in moments of comfort and convenience, but where he stands at times of challenge and controversy'*

Behaviour is usually considered acceptable or unacceptable by others depending on whether or not it interferes with their needs.   This is true when a specific behaviour interferes with the needs of an individual or of a small or a large group. Most socially vetted behaviour stems from this root. Laws are determined by this principle, as is custom and etiquette.

Cultural differences can be ascribed to rules of acceptable behaviour that have evolved in response to differing needs. For example, in Western society, where principles of leadership come from a long and noble tradition, and where society has evolved past tribal traditions to a complex web of power relationships, the act of stepping aside to allow another to pass, and then walking behind them denotes respect and a willingness to 'follow' the other. In tribal Africa however, where physical survival is harsh, the act of walking in front of another denotes great respect because it offers an undefended back. To stand and allow another to walk in front indicates suspicion, and is an insult. Both behaviours stem from the needs of the particular culture and the particular time. Similarly, in China, one would never give anything to anyone else with the left hand, since that is the one that is traditionally used to wipe the bottom. Such a thing would be grossly insulting.

The degree to which behaviour is considered acceptable often depends on many almost arbitrary factors. How we feel often depends on how seriously we regard an infringement of an accepted custom. The young traffic policeman who has just become a father may let a speeding driver off with a caution, while his colleague who has just attended a road traffic accident may 'throw the book at' the driver.

We may also vary our response to a similar situation depending on the 'who', 'where' and 'when' of the incident. A young child will get away with behaviour for which an adult will receive serious censure, and behaviour on Saturday afternoon on the beach is likely to receive a different response on Sunday morning in church!

It is in this arena that prejudice often rears its ugly head. A pretty young woman is frequently allowed to 'get away with' more than an older less attractive man or woman by a male boss, and a black youth is often more closely questioned than his white counterpart when a crime has been committed.

Kogs

I have a dentist friend who works in Sweden. Kogs would consider himself South African, the land of his birth, though is of Indian extraction. Living in the South of Sweden, the family would 'commute' to Copenhagen on the 'flying boat' every now and again for a change of shopping scene. As you probably know, drinking laws are tight in Sweden. Every time the family re-entered their own country, Kogs would be stopped and questioned. His pretty white, blonde, typically Swedish wife said he "looked like a hi-jacker!" Kogs complained, and, to give the Swedish port authorities their due, they did stop singling him out. These are common themes in our cinemas and on our TV screens and reflect a great illness in our society.

Alan

Another example concerns one of our trainee psychotherapists, from Liverpool who told how he had to go to Crown Court to be a witness in a case as part of his work with youths. He asked the court usher which court he should go to regarding the 'Jones' case, and the usher showed him in - into the high-sided box for the accused rather than to the open benches. In actual fact, he was the probation officer in the case. He later told me that he was not entirely surprised at the behaviour of the usher in response to his accent, "After all, all Liverpudlians are perceived as lying, thieving Gits!"

The almost universal tendency to evaluate behaviour in relation to our own needs makes it quite difficult not to think in terms of labels. The driver in front of us who goes slowly when we want to go fast is an "idiot"; the child who makes a noise when we're trying to sleep is a "nuisance", and so on. We've already considered the dangers of using labels. We also saw how our tendency to label others and the type of label we use is more a reflection of ourselves and our relationship to our world and ourselves than a statement about the other person.

If we consider carefully, we will see that the use of a label is almost always a response to the frustration of our needs. This is fairly obvious in the case of the slow driver in front of us, but sometimes we apply labels to people who have little or no direct impact on our lives, such as, the "useless tramp" that we pass in the street. In this case the relationship between our own needs and the label we use is not quite so obvious. However, if we accept that our view of ourselves is predominantly based on the changing reflection of ourselves that we receive back from the world around us then we can start to see that by using this label we may well be responding from a sense of fear or disdain. The tramp's presence represents a threat to our sense of self and our sense of safety. We need security and safety, and the presence of the tramp threatens that, hence our use of the label.

Whose problem?

When we are faced with a difficult situation in which none of the parties seem able or willing to compromise or to delay the fulfilment of their needs, we need to employ other strategies. The first thing to do is to identify the source or ownership of the problem.

In the same way that we are able to change our need to label someone when we can see the situation in terms of how *we* feel, we can begin to resolve a relationship or interaction problem by owning it. Basically, we can identify the ownership of a problem by asking whether the method chosen to fulfil a need conflicts or interferes in any way with another. This sometimes involves ownership of the way we feel as well. If I feel a certain way because someone didn't do something I wanted him or her to do, I am responsible for the way I feel. The fact that I was unable to get someone to act in a way that benefited only me is an inappropriate want, and lack of success is my problem. If I feel a certain way because someone behaved in an inappropriate or unreasonable way towards me, the problem is not mine - the responsibility belongs to the other person. See whether you can understand the difference between when 'self' owns the problem and when 'other' owns the problem in the following examples:

'Self' owns the problem

Derek is frustrated because he can't find his car keys.

June is upset because Sally seemed to ignore her in the canteen.

Matt is angry because his car had a flat tyre and he missed his meeting.

Julia is in pain from a sprained ankle.

'Other' owns the problem

The family has the television up loud while Ann is trying to make a phone call.

George is worried when daughter Jane doesn't arrive home at the agreed time.

Mary doesn't have the stock figures for the meeting because her secretary took an extended lunch and didn't finish typing them up.

Peter is late for work because the boys weren't ready to be dropped at school.

Sometimes there is so much emotional involvement by everyone that it is difficult to distinguish the faint line of difference. Basically, if we feel some way because someone else didn't behave in the way we wanted him or her to behave, but their behaviour is within agreed or

---

EXERCISE 14

WHOSE PROBLEM IS IT?
(Thinking time and then if you can, followed by discussion with others for 20 minutes or so)

PROBLEM OWNERSHIP is one of the most crucial concepts of the **Peace of Mind™** programme. Developing your understanding in this area will help you to approach situations by deciding whose needs need meeting first - the other person's or your own - thereby minimising the risk of becoming so emotionally involved in the other person's problem that you cannot be of any real use.

1. Choosing what to do in situations where others or we get upset is easiest if we are first clear about who owns the problem.

   a) When you are the only one upset by something that is happening or has happened, who owns the problem?

   b) When someone at work is the only one upset by something, now who owns the problem?

   c) When something happens at work to someone that upsets a boss and you, how do you work out who owns the problem?

   If the other person owns the problem, does your getting upset help the situation?

   What can we do to avoid getting upset? Do you use any little tricks to help yourself with this?

   I suggest that you do the following:-

- Ask yourself the question, WHOSE PROBLEM IS IT?

- Ask yourself the question, WHAT'S GOING ON HERE?

- Say to yourself, STOP, LOOK, and LISTEN.

- Breathe out and drop the shoulders.

- Acknowledging your own feelings.

- State to yourself, "I'M FEELING REALLY UPSET" (or whatever your emotion is), then ask:

  "ARE THOSE FEELINGS APPROPRIATE RIGHT NOW?"

RELEVANT POINTS

1. **Emotionally involved versus personally involved.**
   Being emotionally involved usually means taking on the problem and making it our own. This is not the most helpful way to respond to people if they are experiencing a difficulty. It is possible to be personally involved and yet remain detached emotionally. This does not mean you have to be cold and callous!

2. **The importance of leaving responsibility with the other person, even a child, to solve the problem with our help.**

   This in turn:

   - Encourages them to grow emotionally;

   - Encourages their development as SELF RESPONSIBLE people;

   - Requires TRUST that the other person has the intelligence and ability to solve their problem. Many people were not trusted as children and this may make it very difficult to trust other people now. Remember how you felt when you were not trusted to do something you knew you could - how nice it would have been to be trusted more!

   It is useful at this point to think of the idea of how children's dependence on adults varies as they grow (i.e. at O they are 100% dependent and at 18, maybe 0%). Giving them responsibility for aspects of their own lives has to be considered in line with their individual rate of development.

3.   Examples:

- Your child comes home from school upset about a friend's behaviour.

- Your child is playing in front of the T.V. getting in the way of your watching.

- You are worried because your child complains about being bullied at school.

- You are anxious because your child is late home from a friend's house.

- You feel bad when your older child teases the younger one to the point that he gets upset.

- Your child doesn't want to eat what you prepared for her after agreeing to it.

- Your child doesn't want to get dressed when you want to go out.

- Your child squeezes another child very hard while both mothers are there.

The above examples are deliberately chosen to be "small chunk" ones, that is, about youngsters. You can "chunk up" these after you've practised, to your own sometimes more emotionally charged examples.

For each situation pose yourself the following questions:

1.   Whose problem is it?

2.   Whose needs need meeting first?

acceptable bounds, the problem is ours. If however in fulfilling their needs they have 'broken contract' and impinged on our needs, or acted in other broadly unacceptable ways, the problem is theirs.

It sometimes happens that for emotional reasons we 'take on' or become involved in the problems of others. If we attempt to solve them, or assume responsibility for them in an inappropriate way, we impose our solutions on them - in other words, we require them to behave in ways that fill our need to feel good, or do the right thing, or to reduce the discomfort we feel at their problem. Actions such as these are dangerous, and can easily lead to solutions that by our earlier definition are unacceptable.

Prioritising

Sometimes, in spite of all behaviours and responses being correct and reasonable, we are still faced with situations where we have to prioritise and make a sometimes-difficult judgement in order to behave in the most appropriate way.

"When I came upon a road accident, I knew the people needed my help, but I had to deal with my own distress before I could be of any use."

"A week after I had been promoted to manager, I received a list of the redundancies in my division. I was surprised, and more than a little uncomfortable, when Jed, who was on my list, came to see me. He proceeded to tell me about the difficulties he had been having in his marriage, which had finally come to a head, and he was going through a rather messy divorce. He asked for my support. I did what I could to reassure him, but felt awful, and had to see my manager for help in dealing with the situation."

Different people will deal with these situations differently. Most real life situations are complex and require compromise for their resolution. If we are able to separate the problems that belong at our door from the problems that belong elsewhere, we will have gone a long way towards equipping ourselves with the resources required to make complex value judgements like the ones above. We will be able to differentiate between those situations in which our 'help' will become a hindrance because we will recognise our desire to help coming from our own discomfort or a need to be seen to do good. The ability to do this can only improve our life and the lives of those we touch.

A Helping Relationship

We tend to think of a helping relationship only as a professional relationship. Doctors and nurses are trained to help us physically while counsellors, therapists, psychologists and psychiatrists are trained to help us emotionally and mentally. Ironically however, these relationships form a very small part of the total number of relationships we have throughout our lives. The relationships we have with loved ones and colleagues, or even with relative strangers, are more likely to occur at times in our lives when we experience our direst need. The more we exist in a fluid state and respond to situations more often than we react to them, the more likely we are to be of real help to someone else. The more we are able to help one another and the more co-operative we become, the more we will discover that much of the competition and defensiveness around us comes from insecurity and unhappiness. The happier we are, and the happier the people around us, the more peace we will all experience in our lives.

5

Myth and the Mind

The Significance of Myth

Myth and the power of the story has been a part of human civilisation since the dawn of time. Ancient cultures gave special status to their storytellers, who in the days before the written word, were also the historians and the Wise Men or truth-sayers. With our love of science and rationality, we nod our heads sagely, and understand that it was the only way our primitive ancestors had any degree of self-knowledge, or a sense of history. We feel that in our modern times we have no need for frivolity such as stories and mythology.   Only crazy people and children understand the true nature of myth. Bill Moyers in his introduction to the late Joseph Campbell's *"The Power of Myth"* (1988) reflects on Campbell's sentiments (p xii):

"Why do (we) need the mythology?" ... the familiar, modern opinion (is) that "all these Greek gods and stuff" are irrelevant to the human condition today. What ... most do not know - is that the remnants of all that "stuff" line the walls of our interior system of belief, like shards of broken pottery in an archaeological site."

Another believer in the significance of myth to human life was psychologist Carl Gustav Jung. He saw the journey of each individual echoed in the journey of the collective 'hero'. Relegated to the background for a number of years, recent times has seen a resurgence of use of myth - either personal or collective - in the context of personal healing and the fulfilment of human potential, as well as in psychotherapy. The recent interest in meditation, specifically meditation not associated with a particular religion or belief system, or what Hewitt (1992) calls 'Meditation for Better Health and Psycho-Physical Relaxation' has caused a rise in popularity of techniques of 'Creative Visualisation' as well as 'Mind Control'.   The use of altered states of awareness to enhance performance in many spheres - for instance sports performance has also gained a rise in popularity. It may therefore be useful to consider the relationship between myth and the unconscious, and whether we find anything there of value in our quest for **Peace of Mind**.

There are mountains of research data on the nature and function of the two halves or hemispheres of our brain. The differentiation into 'left brain' and 'right brain' is a well-known concept within popular psychology. The left-brain is said to deal with matters of logical and concrete significance, while the right brain is the 'creative' or 'intuitive' side. Following this model, entry into an altered state is said to proceed via the right brain. Techniques of guided visualisation and mind control use the creative faculty of the mind to change attitudes and destructive beliefs in life. In the words of Marilee Zdenek, in her book *"The Right Brain Experience"* (1983, p 60):

"How can anyone rise above a limitation that is self-imposed? The internal judge has the last word. ... Two conditions are essential for success; positive thinking and positive feeling. The first is a product of your analytical self; the second is a product of your emotional self."

If this is true, and our experience and the experience of many others says that it is - then two things are necessary to bring about change - there needs to be a change in thought and belief as well as change in feeling. So how can this be achieved? A change in thinking seems possible - we can change our minds, and almost all that we have discussed so far relates changing the way we think about ourselves. Modern psychotherapy has shown that it is possible to bring about tremendous change using techniques that access only the conscious part of the brain. But these changes are slow, and in most instances require the presence of another human being. After all, it is not very satisfactory to talk to a wall (as Shirley Valentine proved! (Russell 1988)). So, reading this book, all alone, with nothing but a wall for company, we clearly need to work not only on the mental level, but also on the emotional level. So how are we to do this? Emotions, or certainly that which influences them, seems to be beyond our conscious control. The way we feel seems to come from somewhere very deep inside, somewhere from that dark and shady place psychology calls the unconscious. Some feelings are easier to change than others. Sometimes it is possible to lift our mood or state of mind by changing our thoughts, but some feelings are so basic and profound that we can't seem to reach them.

Mental Imaging - The Theory

There is a technique called 'mental imaging' by the academic establishment. Positive results have come from research into this technique. Syer and Connolly (1984) list the following benefits of Mental Imaging:

1. It affects physical functioning - research into biofeedback techniques has demonstrated the ability of the mind to do this.

2. It accelerates the learning process - physical practise involves nerve impulses running from muscles to the brain. This widens the pathway between muscles and brain used by these signals, in a similar way to the way a path is worn across the field by many walkers. Mental imaging has been found to cause a similar effect - therefore mental practise can be very powerful and as useful as physical practise.

3. It uses a language the body understands. The body does not communicate by words, it communicates by seeing and feeling - visually / kinaesthetically.

Syer & Connolly (p.47) go on to say:

"Visualisation is a skill. It is the process of watching yourself on a screen in your mind's eye, consciously evoking and guiding daydreams in which you appear, usually towards a specific end. The academic term for this technique is mental imaging. We keep the common usage 'visualisation', but it is important to remember that visualisation includes an auditory and kinaesthetic (feeling) component. In other words, if you visualise yourself moving, you may see, hear and feel yourself moving. In most visualisation the kinaesthetic sense is particularly important."

Although these words were written a while ago, and with sports performance in mind, they remain essentially true and relevant to other aspects of life as well. Visualisation is essentially a right brain, or creative exercise, and as such, may prove a bit of a challenge to the many of us who function predominantly using our left-brain. It is a challenge and not an impossibility, and in fact quite easy via states of altered awareness, which will be discussed at great length in Part II. The 'challenge' part lies in being able to remain 'open' to ideas which may be totally foreign to us, and which we may consider a waste of time.

There is a great deal 'out there' about and surrounding what is commonly called visualisation techniques, and much of it is associated with rather 'spaced out' and alternative philosophies. To ignore the proven value of such techniques on the basis of possible questionable associations is of the order of tossing out the baby with the bath water. The sensible course is to keep an open mind, but not quite so open that our brains fall out!

Keeping our brains (both left and right) safely in their place, let us return to the idea of myth, with which we began this chapter. Myth is really nothing more than a symbolic communication on a collective or general scale.   Communication that comes out of the individual unconscious seems to be in the form of symbols (for example dreams) so it makes sense to use the same terminology to communicate in the other direction. Early man used myth to make sense of his world, and different cultures used different myths to describe the same events. Take the myth of creation - the Babylonians told of, "The Epic of Gilgamesh". In it, the world is made of water, and Gilgamesh sets off to slay the chaos dragon. He eventually kills it and cuts it in half, putting half of it below his feet, the earth - and the other half above his head as the firmament, or heaven. Many of us are more familiar with the Jewish or Biblical version, wherein God created heaven and earth in seven days. Myth and stories were also used to explain human behaviour.   The Greeks used Pandora's box to explain the presence of trouble and difficulties in daily life. The Jews used Eve's taking the fruit from the tree of knowledge of good and evil in an attempt to explain the presence of hardship in life. The slaying of Abel by Cain, likewise, was the attempt to explain murder in our society.   The Tower of Babel was taught to explain why humans had different tongues, and Abram and his children by Sarah and Hagar the two major religions of the time of Judaism and Islaam.

The use of myth in ancient and traditional 'psychology' establishes a good precedent for us to follow. It is probably worthwhile to take the time to learn the symbolic language of the unconscious. By beginning to understand the messages that come from the unconscious - both our own, in the form of dreams and images, and that from the minds of others, through the use of world myth and fairytale - we can begin to formulate messages from our conscious to our unconscious.

Much interesting work has grown out of Jung's theories. One in particular springs to mind, and that is the work of Dora Kalff from Germany. She is the pioneer of what has come to be called 'Sandplay Therapy', which consists of constructing a picture or scene in a sand tray. Toys and symbols are used to create a picture in the sand. Recorded over time, these pictures or images produce a fascinating window on the hidden part of the mind, and the process of their creation has a powerful therapeutic effect on the psyche. The basis of the therapy is non-verbal, and the role of the therapist is as witness and support for the unfolding journey of the client.

Mental images can be used in a similar way. Each of us has our own story or myth, which we are enacting in our lives. When our lives 'don't work' for whatever reason, we can help ourselves to cope better by discovering the reason for our difficulty and by recognising that our lives are in effect our own hero's journey. Our difficulty may stem from 'faulty programming' or inappropriate ideas we hold about ourselves, usually dating from a distant childhood time; from too much stress; ill health, or any of a number of problems which can beset us on our journey.

The following inner journey with Joan came up and occurred spontaneously within a therapy session. It is an example of how individual a symbolic journey can be, and also how powerful. If we accept the research finding reported by Syer & Connolly, that nerve pathways are widened by the use of mental techniques, then it is easy to see that a mythical or symbolic journey like this does in fact 'get into' a real place somewhere in the hidden part of ourselves, and can in fact influence our lives tremendously.

Joan

Joan is a very self-aware individual - someone who has spent a large portion of her life looking at the reasons her life is the way it is. Although she doesn't believe in pre-destiny as such, some of the events in her life, and her apparent powerlessness in the face of them makes her tend towards the idea of karmic retribution - or that somehow the misfortunes in her life may be a kind of a repayment for 'previous' wrongs.

Before seeking help in her personal explorations, Joan had concluded that much of her sense of not being quite connected to the events in her life stemmed from a gap in her very early years. She was adopted at the age of three months, after apparently having been somewhat neglected by her teenage mother. Her adoptive parents were wonderful, and she grew up secure in the knowledge of her specialness and of how dearly she was loved and wanted.

A single, very dark cloud on the horizon was the fact that her biological parents were not married. She discovered that she was illegitimate at the age of about 9, when she understood the full implications of this fact. To her, at nine years old, illegitimate meant 'not legal'. Illegitimate meant 'no right to be here'.

Suddenly to the adult Joan it became very clear that her lifelong insecurity and shyness was related to the idea of not really having a right to take up the space she occupied. She also made the interesting connection that her frequent complicated dealings with lawyers and the legal system over the purchase of houses and so on echoed the idea that she was 'not legal.'

Using mental imaging, or creative visualisation, Joan placed herself on a sunny mountainside in front of the entrance to a dark cave. Gingerly she entered the cave, and armed herself with armour from the armoury at the entrance to the cave.

Suitably protected, she took the flaming torch from the wall and proceeded down a dark passage. The floor was sloping downwards, and each step took her deeper and deeper into the bowels of the earth, and further and further away from the safe sunshine outside. The incline became steeper and steeper downwards, till she reached a series of stairs cut into the rock. She started down the stairs, and discovered that on each step a letter was carved. Going from step to step, she soon saw that the steps read 'ILLEGITIMATE'. Stepping off the last step, she found her passage blocked by a small locked door.

Determined, she managed to pry the door open, and inside she found a small room, stacked to the ceiling with cardboard boxes. On each box was written an attribute that had caused her distress throughout her life. She saw 'no confidence', 'useless', 'ugly', ''no right' and many more.

Each box seemed to be suspended from the ceiling by a white cord, and it seemed important to her that the first thing she do is to disconnect these boxes from the cords that bound them, and using the sword with which she had armed herself, she set about cutting the boxes free.

When she had done that, she was satisfied, and didn't feel the need to go any further at that stage, so she left the room and found, to her delight that the word spelled by the steps had changed to 'LEGITIMATE', and that each step upwards was an uplifting experience, where her legs became stronger, and her heart became bolder. Finally she reached the sunny mountainside, and sat there for a while, enjoying the bright sunshine after the dark dankness of the cave.

After her inner journey, Joan reported feeling a great deal brighter and happier. She was also aware that she wanted to go back to the little room, because she wanted to look inside some of the boxes, and probably even destroy them.

For now she felt that having cut the white cords that bound them together, and probably to her life, she could choose the time she would go back and 'finish the job'.

There are of course universal journeys - and Joan's journey contained some universal elements. It is easy to identify some of these, such as the downward movement, and the protection by magical weapons - but they also served a pragmatic purpose. And so it is with most personal mythological stores.

Popular Fantasy, both films and books really reflect a desire to access our symbolic selves. The simple reality is that we can access our deepest parts, and bring about profound changes as quickly and simply as Joan did.

Affirmations

One more thing that must be mentioned here is the power and use of verbal instructions. Psychotherapists call the use of words in this way 'ego strengthening'. Others speak simply of affirmations. Louise Hay has written whole books on the subject of changing our perceptions of ourselves by changing the way we think about ourselves, and she suggests the use of visualisation together with affirmations, because the one strengthens the other. So what exactly is an affirmation? Stuart Wilde (1987, p16) proposes the following definition:

"An affirmation is, in effect, a statement either of word, thought, feeling, or action that underlines or confirms a belief pattern that you hold. There are negative or positive affirmations."

This is by no means new. Those of us who have either read John Galsworthy's "The Forsyte Saga" of which the first novel was published in 1906, or who are old enough to remember it on British television, will remember the rather lovely child of our hero, Soames Forsyte. As a mother-to-be (ignorant of what we know of modern genetics) she wanders around saying to herself, repetitively and monotonously, "Each day, in every way, my child is becoming more and more male". The French Doctor Emile Coué, who wrote "Self Mastery Through Autosuggestion" (1922) was in fashion at the time, and purported that the monotonous repetition of desired outcomes in this fashion would have the desired effect. He advocated a string with twenty little knots in it, on the way to sleep at night and first thing whilst waking up in the morning to use the phrase 'EACH DAY IN *EVERY* WAY I AM GETTING BETTER AND BETTER'. He has it printed like this, in capitals, to emphasise the importance of his suggestion.

An affirmation may confirm a belief that is already held, or it may seek to reinforce a belief that is preferred to the one that is currently held. If we have no confidence in ourselves, and the merest thought of talking to a stranger makes us quiver, we do so because we believe that we are basically worthless. We may choose an affirmation something like, 'With every passing moment I feel more and more confident' or 'I am a valuable and unique person'.

We will look at the specifics of the way we can use affirmations to enhance our lives in Part II.

6

Stress

Enough has been written on the subject of stress to fill more than one sizeable library. The fact that many companies now employ 'Stress Busters' to help their employees cope with stress is a positive step forward, but is also in itself a sad indictment of the state we find ourselves in. In many respects, stress has recently been 'discovered', and there are not many who would now argue the figures put out on a regular basis claiming enormous percentage loss in profits to companies due to the effects of stress on employees. As stress is clearly one of the great obstacles to peace of mind, it is necessary to consider it here, under a separate heading, although even without specific attention being paid to it, stress levels automatically reduce when life is lived more effectively and peacefully. All of the various aspects presented within **Peace of Mind** have an impact on the level of stress experienced by the individual. When personal, internal stress is reduced (via relaxation) and psychological tensions are reduced (via self-hypnosis, visualisation and affirmations) and interpersonal stress is reduced (via more effective communications and positive relationships) 'stress' as a separate entity no longer exists.

So saying, it is useful to consider what Mihaly Csikszentmihalyi (1992) says on the subject in his book *"Flow - The Psychology of Happiness"*. He takes, and frequently reiterates the view that it is not external fortune or misfortune that determines how a given individual will cope, but the inner resources and ultimately the belief system of that individual. If we believe that we are the victims of our circumstances, we will experience our lives as exceedingly stressful. Gaining power or control over our lives is not however enough to remove the negative effects of stress. Pursuing the positive or 'flow' of human experience - that experience during which awareness of self and time are lost, Csikszentmihalyi throws light on the reasons we experience the events or circumstances in our lives as stressful.

He traces the way that agencies that seek powers for specific purposes - states, churches, employers, retailers and many more, exploit human consciousness and control human behaviour to their own ends. His definition of stress is that it occurs when the individual looses control their life, resulting in a belief that they are essentially powerless. His solution is for the individual to regain their perceived loss of power. Many of us try to do this by changing our external life circumstances, perhaps by, getting a new job, moving house, having children or getting married or divorced. Unfortunately, Csikszentmihalyi says that this will not remove the source of stress, because by fulfilling what are probably our "heart's desires" we are actually further "buying in" to the system that is controlling us and was the cause of our stress in the first place. For him the solution lies in our ability to control our consciousness awareness. He says (p. 19):

> "The most important step in emancipating oneself from social controls is the ability to find rewards in the events of each moment. If a person learns to enjoy and find meaning in the ongoing stream of experience, in the process of living itself, the burden of social controls automatically falls from one's shoulders. Power returns to the person when rewards are no longer relegated to outside forces".

Whether or not we agree with this view, it offers a credible explanation for the process by which stress occurs. First of all, it must be understood that stress itself is not negative.   On a physical level, movement is only possible *because* of stress. Muscles pulling or working against each other make it possible for us to move our limbs. "We know about that stress", we may say. "That's different".

Diagram to show the origin of stress due both to over and under-stimulation

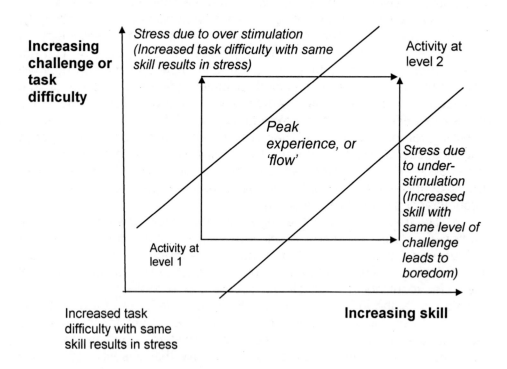

The diagram shows how both too much pressure and too little pressure can cause stress. It is important to remember this when looking at the nature of stress.

If we consider the stress endured by say an Olympic sprinter who runs 100 meters, compared to that required by a 50 year old, sedentary business man to perform the same feat, the businessman would report extreme discomfort and stress, while the sprinter would probably report a peak experience!

Clearly then, what we can call negative stress is specific to a particular individual at a particular time.   So we could define negative stress as the experience of individual discomfort due to circumstances, external or internal, that are beyond the coping capacity or style of that individual. The key to coping with stress is therefore either to increase the ability to cope or reduce the stressful stimuli. Csikszentmihalyi's solution would fall into the first category.   In an effort to change external circumstances, we may consider the following model, adapted from Csikszentmihalyi's book (p.74).

Penny Moon, gifted psychotherapist and teacher identifies 5 separate sources of stress in our lives. The following tables are from her stress management package, and reproduced with her kind permission. Her categories are as follows:-

Some Causes of Stress

CHEMICAL	EMOTIONAL	STRUCTURAL
• Insufficient water • Poor diet & nutritional deficiencies • Food & /or environmental allergies • Heavy metal toxicity Impure water and air Agricultural sprays • Genetic biochemical defects.	• Past emotional traumas • Current & future worries & anxieties • Fears, phobias, self-esteem issues • Lack of belief system • Fear of failure &/or success Past programming	• Muscular-skeletal stress • Physical trauma - e.g. whiplash • Inappropriate, insufficient or over exercise • Poor posture • Maladjustment in work place • Shallow breathing

BEHAVIOURAL	ENVIRONMENTAL
• Inadequate sleep and rest • Use & abuse of "recreational" and medicinal drugs • Dysfunctional family background • Perfectionism • Procrastination • Workaholism • Poor time management • Organisational skills	• Sensitivity to florescent lighting • Sensitivity (allergy) to specific colours • Sensitivity to noise, radiation & electro-magnetic pollution

The signs of over-stress are as many and as varied as the people exhibiting them. What is not in dispute about stress is the effects it can have on our lives, and the extent to which it can cause physical as well as emotional and mental illness. Penny's list offers an eye-opening and sobering focus for the evaluation of our own state of stress.

Signs and Symptoms of Stress

MENTAL & EMOTIONAL	PHYSICAL	BEHAVIOURAL
• Giving up • Poor memory • Making mistakes • Feeling helpless • Reduced control • Inability to relax • Losing enthusiasm • Sleep disturbance • Losing self esteem • Becoming resentful • Taking offence easily	• Migraine • Sweating • Allergies • Headaches • Chest pains • Skin irritations • Stomach problems • Heart palpitations • Acidity & indigestion • Muscular aches & pains • Irritable bowel syndrome	• Lethargy • Isolation • Fidgeting • Nervous habits • Procrastination • Irrational decisions • Showing disapproval • Moodiness & grudges • Being less co-operative • Accidents & clumsiness • Taking time off work

• Flying off the handle • Losing sense of humour • Difficulty with decision making • Becoming suspicious and unhelpful • Reduced interest and concentration	• Constant colds and other infections	• Interrupting conversations • Poor personal presentation • Talking, eating & walking quickly • Increases in drinking, smoking & eating

The degree to which we exhibit some or any of these symptoms is a function of the degree to which we are affected by stress. Part of the solution lies in identifying the source of the stress and working towards brining pressures to acceptable levels. The other part of dealing with stress, as we have already said, is strengthening ourselves to cope with pressures. This may involve doing as Csikszentmihalyi suggests, which is expanding or extending the level of our consciousness, or by strengthening ourselves in another way.

"All very well", you may say, "but what can I do in a practical sense about the stresses that affect my daily life?" First of all, by changing our view of ourselves and being kinder and more accepting of ourselves, we automatically relieve some internal pressures at an emotional level. Some of the ideas and techniques discussed in the second part of this book will help you to do this. In addition, there are also things that we can do to relieve stress at the physical level, in particular by looking after ourselves, making sure that we get a proper and wholesome diet, as well as, sufficient exercise and sleep. Also, the use of alternative therapies and massage to help our bodies deal with the effects of stress can be extremely effective ways of helping to maintain a sense of balance and well being. But perhaps the best and most useful technique is of course prevention. Remember that stress is not possible where there is **Peace of Mind**.

Part II: So What Can I Do?

7

Relationship with the Self

Part two is more of a practical nature than part one, but rather that give specific exercises to be done in a specific order for a specific purpose, I have chosen a wider approach. I believe passionately in two things. Firstly, in the power and the right of the individual, not only to know what's best for them self, but also to do what's necessary for their own best interest. Secondly, that no two sets of circumstances are the same, and that our particular path through the universe is uniquely our own.

Our particular solution is ours only, and cannot belong to anyone else. Consequently, following the principle that to give a man a fish feeds him for one day, whilst teaching him to fish feeds him for the rest of his life, I aim to offer, with love, the tools that I have found to be of use in my life and in the lives of those that I have worked with. The choice and responsibility of how exactly they are used belongs to you, the reader, and cannot be dictated by words on a page.

Stress

As we have seen, stress in itself is a necessary part of life. The problem comes when the stress we experience is more than we can cope with. If we are experiencing unacceptably high levels of stress, and we have the power to change our circumstances, the best way is to remove ourselves from the source of our discomfort. Most often, however, our ability to reduce the stress 'coming at us' is quite limited.

We may not immediately be able to afford the luxury of changing a stressful job, or of getting 'someone in' to help us cope. What we're left with then is to do what we can to increase our ability to cope, a bit like the way we would check and service our car before setting out on an extra long journey. We have looked at some of the ways we can begin to get in touch with the inner parts of ourselves in Part 1. We will now look at some techniques that have proved useful to many different people over the years.

Altered Awareness

First of all, how can altering our awareness be useful to us - how can that help us achieve greater **Peace of Mind** and help us cope with the circumstances we find in our lives? The best advice is to adopt a 'suck it and see' approach. Each person must and will choose their own path for themselves. The information given in this volume is based on the collective experience of a group of similarly minded people, who have gained great benefits from these ideas and techniques over many collective years of living and therapeutic practise. I offer it with the assurance that it has worked well for me.

Making use of techniques of altered awareness has two distinct benefits. In the first place it enables deep relaxation of both body and mind, and relaxation at this level is a powerful antidote to the stress of daily living. When the body is able to cope with stress, it does not need to display the host of symptoms we have given the collective term 'dis-ease.'

The second profound benefit of altered awareness work is that it allows access to deeper parts of ourselves, and because it partially by-passes the 'critical factor' in our personality - the computer operator/programmer that we referred to in Part I, it becomes possible, by the use of affirmations or positive statements about ourselves, to influence many of the attitudes and beliefs we so often hold. This is a very pragmatic and useful way of influencing our general well being.

When our belief about ourselves changes, our behaviour changes, and the new behaviour reinforces our 'new' belief, which accelerates positive change in an upward spiral way, just as the original negative beliefs were reinforced in a downward spiral. In many cases these negative beliefs were established while we were young - before the 'critical factor' part of our personality was fully developed. Indeed, a large part of this 'critical factor' owes its existence to the very negative attitudes that cause us discomfort in our daily living.

So what exactly do we mean by 'altered awareness? A good way to gain some perspective on what has different names (all of them emotive!) is to consider it in an historical context. The study and practise of altered awareness is one of the most ancient of human practises. Traditionally it has been associated with religions or cultural belief systems. In societies that we sometimes call primitive, 'special' members of communities were either taught during the course of a usually lengthy apprenticeship to achieve a state of altered awareness from which would emerge benefits for the community at large. Sometimes this process was assisted by consuming mind altering plants or plant extracts, and sometimes it was a process in which the whole community participated. The ability to enter an altered state, or even to appear to enter an altered state conferred great power, and in many cases this resulted in 'power over' the masses, with 'information' being received from the current divinity while in this state. In some cultures there was a greater devolution of this power, and individuals were able to work towards achieving this altered state ability. In many North American Indian cultures, for example, it was the norm for each member of the community to seek out their own truth on a 'vision quest', sometimes assisted by mind altering substances. This vision quest almost always included many of the aspects of self development covered in this volume - exploration of the self, both the self from the past and the self in the present.

In the East, the tradition turned more to the establishment of groups of students or disciples who studied under a Master or teacher - quite literally someone who had mastered all states of being. In the West we initially adopted this approach as well by following the teachings of one or other Master teacher.

As pure science gained in power and popularity, so we began to move away from belief in the usefulness, or even the existence of an altered state of mind. Studies that were conducted were basically flawed from the start, because it is impossible to experience a mind state in the physical sense, and the debate began, attempting to
locate the mind in the physical brain. Ancient practises of meditation were discredited as belonging to heathen religions and research such as there was into the scientific basis for altered awareness hung on the fringes or respectability.

And in spite of huge advances in scientific study, in the minds of many this is still a fairly basic belief. Let us now, with the aid of some layman's science, attempt to explain what has been discovered about 'altered awareness'.

EEG (or electroencephalograph) readings have shown four basic types of brainwave pattern in the human brain. These are patterns of electric discharge by the neurones in the brain. Over many studies they have found that certain waves are most often associated with certain activities. Alpha and Beta waves occur mainly during waking, and Theta and Delta waves occur during sleep. Beta waves are the fastest, and show up as short spiky squiggles on the graph. Delta waves are the slowest, and occur during deep, unconscious sleep, or unconsciousness. Between these two extremes lie Alpha and Theta waves. Of the two, Theta waves are slower, and are found during sleep. Alpha waves occur during the threshold period between ordinary wakefulness and regular sleep. When practising altered awareness, the EEG measures Alpha waves, and the slower the wave, the deeper the state of mental relaxation - or usually the 'more pleasant' the experience of altered awareness is reported to be on a subjective level.

Other changes occur to the physiology when in this state that have been proved to be most beneficial, and of the order of increasing the body's ability to deal with external stresses. One of the key elements of altered state awareness, which will be discussed further in a moment, is an alteration in breathing rate. Now without going into an unnecessary lesson on the biological structure of nerves and the nervous system, it is enough to state that as breathing becomes slower, there is less exchange of gasses in the lungs, and the level of carbon dioxide in the blood stream increases. Nerve impulses are transmitted along a series of nerve fibres, which are long stringy fibres running through the body, and massed in the brain. There are little gaps between the fibres, and these gaps are filled with chemical substances called neurotransmitters. A nerve impulse is a change in the small electrical polarity of the outside of the nerve relative to the inside of the nerve cell. When a nerve impulse starts - in other words, when this wave of polarity change starts along the length of a nerve - it cannot stop until it reaches the end of the nerve. This is where the little gaps between the nerve fibres come in. If there were no gaps, it would be impossible to have relief from pain for example, because the transmission of the pain impulse would race along these nerves and be experienced as pain at the other end. When the change in polarity reaches the gap between nerves, it has to hop across, literally on the back of the chemical carriers. If for some reason the body (or the doctor, via the introduction of a chemical) does not want the nerve impulse to be transmitted, it changes the nature of the chemical in the gap. Some chemicals act as inhibitors of the nerve impulse, while others act as transmitters.

At the risk of simplifying to absurdity what is a vastly complex chemical process, we can say that a change in the gas levels in the blood - in this case increased carbon dioxide - sets up a chain of messages that results in nerve impulses being blocked or retarded.

It is important to realise that the nervous system operates on a principle of 'all or nothing'. In other words a nerve impulse does not fire a little bit. It either fires or does not. So if you receive a pin prick, the nerve impulses fire as completely as they do if you receive a huge gash in your arm with blood spurting everywhere. The difference is that with the pinprick, only a few nerves out of the millions of possible nerves that serve that area, respond. With a more massive trauma, many more nerves are activated, and so the pain is experienced as intense.

How this principle affects altered state awareness is that as we relax more and more deeply, and our breathing gets deeper and slower, more and more nerves 'don't fire', so we are less and less bothered by external stimuli, such as noises for instance. We still hear them, and they are as loud as ever, but they no longer bother us. This chemical process also makes possible the loss of body sensation so often reported. As the body relaxes and seems to 'float away', greater and greater relaxation is achieved, with its attendant benefits.

We have used the term 'altered awareness' to describe this state to avoid the emotive alternatives 'meditation', 'hypnosis' or 'auto-hypnosis'. In reality the processes are the same, both in terms of physical responses and in terms of subjective experience. And there is a growing body of evidence to suggest that regular experience of the deep physical and mental relaxation that occurs during this state has vast benefits to both mental and physical health. Hewitt (1992, p. 18) says:

"The good news has spread that meditation improves physical and mental health, principally by releasing stress. Medical scientists have investigated the physiological and psychological changes produced by the practice of meditation and found that it elicits a 'Relaxation Response' that is the opposite of the fight-or flight response to danger."

It would be easy to enumerate the listed benefits of meditation - for each writer on the subject has a list of personal favourites, and these would include items such as "better sleep", "more energy", "greater mental clarity". These and many more may well be the consequence of adopting regular meditation practise. Be aware however that in as much as we are all unique, and our circumstances are pretty much unique, our response will be unique as well, and may or may not conform to some generalised list of benefits. Again we suggest trying out and finding the one or ones that are best suited.

There are so many approaches to meditation or hypnosis that we find ourselves lost in a maze of confusion. Quite simply, there are only **three things** necessary to enter an altered state - whether we choose to call that state meditation or hypnosis. Our intent once we enter that state is pretty much what makes the difference. Traditionally meditation has as its focus the 'raising' of consciousness. Words such as 'expanded awareness' or 'inclusiveness' or 'unity consciousness' are used to describe states of mind, while words such as 'compassion', 'love' and 'brotherhood' are applied to relationships and interactions. Physical benefits are often seen as useful side effects to the main objective. The focus of those who prefer the term 'auto-hypnosis' is more likely to be to improve the immediate physical circumstances - to stop a bad habit, to lose weight, to increase self-confidence, or to reduce stress. Altered awareness is a sometimes-unnoticed side effect.

The good news is that these two objectives are not mutually exclusive. An analogy to the process would be shining a torch beam in the dark. The fact that the beam focuses on one point does not mean that nothing but the circle of light exists. The beam of light is no more than our belief system. And we do not need to have a belief system in order to gain the benefits promised.

As we've said, there are only three very simple requirements for an altered mental state. They are **narrowed focus of attention,** an **altered breathing pattern** and **monotony**. Let us explore these more fully.

Narrowed Focus of Attention

In traditional hypnosis practise this either involves counting or visually focusing on a particular spot. Counting down usually begins with a fairly high number, such as 300, so that counting downwards involves a little bit of mental effort. This effort effectively reduces external "interference" by random thoughts. Instructions for focusing on a single spot - such as a spot on the ceiling, or a burning candle flame usually includes specific instructions such as "do not let your eyes wander away for a moment, and if they do, bring them back again, and keep them focused there".

The practise of meditation often involves the use of a mantra - a word of either no significance, or of specific religious significance. Constant repetition of this word or sound again brings the mind into focus, and reduces random thoughts. Some meditation uses a sound vocalised externally - usually a sound such as "Ah", or "Aum" (pronounced as "Om"), which sets up a physical vibration in the throat and chest, which once again deepens the process.

Another system often used is progressive relaxation. By paying attention to each group of muscles, and either tensing, then relaxing them, or simply by being aware of them, all extraneous thoughts and distractions are eliminated, and a narrowed focus of attention is achieved. Another method is to focus on sensory experience - sound for instance, and the instruction may be to become aware of sounds in the distance, then sounds in the room, then sounds within the body itself - leading to focus on the flow of breath.

Altered Breathing Patterns

Physical induction methods usually bring the focus of attention to the process of breathing at some point, and the instruction is to become aware of the flow of breath in and out of the body. This act of focus is enough to alter the rate of breathing, even when the instruction is to breathe naturally and comfortably. Other systems may focus on breath from the beginning, and ask the subject to count each in and out breath, thereby deliberately controlling the rate of breathing. This combines focus of attention and altered breathing in one. This technique is a favourite in the practise of yoga, where prana, or breath quite literally means life force, and control of this is considered to be of great benefit. Where a mantra is used, repetition of the mantra soon falls into the pattern of breathing, and this focus slows breathing.

As we have seen, this slowing of breath is vital to the process of deep relaxation, because it produces a higher concentration of carbon dioxide in the blood, which in turn further activates the relaxation response.

Monotony

This is clearly present in all the techniques. The process of breathing is in itself a monotonous one. Use of a mantra increases monotony as we have seen. The exact technique we choose depends on what works for us. We may prefer to use a technique that we can 'get' from somewhere - a book, or a tape, or we may choose to construct our own, using the three simple principles outlined above. When we begin, if we have never tried to meditate, or enter a state of altered awareness before, the process may seem slow and laborious, but the good news is that like learning anything else, the more we practise, the easier it gets. Eventually it becomes possible to enter a deep altered state with a simple exhalation of breath or by the use of some other trigger. For now, let us practise achieving this state for ourselves, and become aware of what it 'feels like' once we get there. Then we will look at what we can do once we're there, and to what benefit.

Induction or Entering an Altered State

Here are some possible scripts for a few of the induction techniques discussed: There are of course many more methods, and all of them equally effective, as long as they contain the basic ingredients for altered awareness, as discussed.

"Sound of Calm" Induction

This is an adaptation for self-hypnosis from the "Sound of Calm" technique used by Sue Washington and her staff at Centre Training International School of Hypnotherapy and Psychotherapy.

The Centre Training Method is in turn adapted from the version taught by Dr D.W. Ebrahim. Dr Ebrahim used material taught him by the late Dr. John Hartland, MD.

As with all the following inductions, read the script through a few times, then put the book aside and go through the procedure in your mind, being careful to include all steps.

1. Make yourself comfortable - best sitting up, with your head supported behind you. Look straight ahead, then let your eyes wander upwards to a spot on the ceiling or above your normal eye level. It can be a real spot or an imaginary spot. Focus unwaveringly on this spot as you........

2. Begin to count backwards in your head, not out loud, from 300. When you reach 295 let your eyes close... let your eyelids feel heavy and limp.

3. Then repeat the word CALM in your head, not out loud, but gently with each breath you breathe out.... CALM.... CALM... Don't give it any meaning, just repeat it as a sound, like the sound of a distant bell in your head... And with each breath out, and each time you repeat the sound of calm, become aware that your mind and body are becoming calm.

4. Let the heaviness and relaxation from your eyelids flow up through your eyebrows, over your forehead, over the top of your head and down the back of your head and neck.

5. Let the heaviness and relaxation flow down your face, down your cheeks and nose, round your mouth and chin and down the front of your neck as you allow the weight of your head to sink into the support of the pillow or cushion behind it.

6. Feel the relaxation spread to your back muscles, as they become limp and slack and heavy

7. Become aware of your chest muscles, and the progressive relaxation of the muscles there, as your breathing becomes easier and more gentle and more natural.

8. Let your shoulders go, slump down limp and slack and heavy, and let that heaviness and relaxation flow down through your arms.... your upper arms and elbows, lower arms and wrists, hands and fingers, down to the tips of your fingers.

9. And then downwards through your trunk....and let that relaxation flow down round your waist, down through your tummy ....down through your bottom and all the way round your hips ... down through your upper legs and thighs, knees, lower legs, ankles and feet, down to the very tiniest muscles at the end of your toes.

(Appendix 1 on page 147 contains the full version of this text. It is TRACK 1 on the CD).

Counting Induction

This is the induction used by José Silva in the Silva Mind Control Method (From You the Healer, by *Silva and Stone,* HJ Kramer Inc, 1989).

As part of self-training, Silva suggests a 40 day programme of twice daily relaxation, based on counting downwards in order to lead the mind into a very relaxed 'alpha' state ("Alpha" refers to a specific level of brainwave frequency associated with being in a relaxed state).

The idea is to gently focus the mind on counting backwards as a means of slowing it right down into a state of deep relaxation. With practice the length of time that is required to achieve an alpha state reduces, so that for the first 10 days counting proceeds from 100 down to 1; during the second 10 days from 50 to 1; during the third 10 days from 25 to 1, and for the final 10 days from 10 to 1.

Silva's first instruction is to close the eyes and roll them slightly upwards, towards the eyebrows, then to begin the countdown, waiting about 1 second between each count.

Hewitt (1992) suggests that the counting begins at 10 and goes down to 1, and that each count is on the out breath. When you reach 1, you start again at 10, and continue the process, gradually taking the mind down into deeper levels of relaxation.

Progressive muscle relaxation

1. Concentrate on relaxing. Breathe slowly and deeply and say the word "relax" to yourself in your mind as you breathe out.
2. Make your hands into tight fists, then, let them relax. Tense the muscle groups in your arms, one at a time, then, let them relax. Tense the muscles of your feet and legs, and let them relax. Continue with the muscles all over your body - either beginning at one end and working progressively, or working from where the tension is most obvious.
3. Continue to be as aware as possible of breathing, and consciously allow the tension from each group of relaxed muscles to flow away, leaving your body deeply relaxed with each breath that you breathe out.

Sensory Focus Induction

1. Make yourself comfortable, and allow yourself to begin to relax. Become aware of your breathing, as you breathe in and out and in and out.
2. Then become aware of sounds outside of the room - both distant sounds and near sounds. Allow your awareness to linger, effortlessly on what you can hear.
3. Bring the focus of attention back into the room. Be aware of sounds inside the room - a clock ticking, or the roar of the silence if there are no sounds at all.
4. Become aware of sensations closer to the body - the way your body contacts the surface you are lying / sitting on; the sensation where your clothes touch you; hair lying on your forehead; cool or warm air on the skin - anything near or around the body.
5. Then turn focus to inside the body. Become aware of movement inside the body - heart beat - the flow of blood in the veins; movement in the digestive canal; the flow of the breath, in and out. Stay with the breath - stay with one breath - feel it as it touches the nose - cold on the nostrils; feel it go down all the way to the bottom of the lungs; experience the slight pause there, then the rush as it flows up and out again, the out breath slightly warmer than the in breath.
6. After a while, stay with the nostrils, and feel only the difference in temperature between the out and the in breath. Become aware of the difference to the nostrils between the breath and the gap between the breath. Become aware of the stillness. And allow yourself to relax into it. Totally still and peaceful.

An important thing to bear in mind when practising any of these inductions is that they are beginnings - they help us to reach a state of deep relaxation. It is as important to know how to come out of the state of relaxation as it is to know how to go into it. One option is to use one of these techniques before going to sleep - to give yourself the instruction that the deep relaxation will turn into deep and comfortable sleep.

A word of warning though - this type of deep relaxation may have an energising effect. The case of a 70+ year old comes to mind. It was suggested that when she had trouble fitting the technique into her daily routine, that she may give it a shot on the way to bed at night. Her retort was, "Oh, I couldn't possibly do that. After my meditation, I feel so energised, I'd have to get up and clean the kitchen before I could go to bed!" Perhaps a better option is to come out of the state of deep relaxation before going to sleep.

It is as simple to come out of relaxation as it is to enter it. If specific instructions were used - such as your muscles are getting heavier and heavier, then the process must be repeated, but in reverse. Muscles should begin to feel lighter and lighter - or the heaviness must leave the muscles. In autohypnosis or meditation, the instructions will obviously not be verbal. The initial sense of heaviness in the muscles must be countered by a sensation of lightness in the muscles. It is usually enough to bring awareness back into the present by becoming aware of the body again, perhaps focusing on physical sensation - in effect grounding the experience back in body awareness.

Practise the induction and the process of coming out of the altered state regularly, and when the process is easy and comfortable, we can begin to explore the 'what next' options.

8

A Better Relationship with the Self

Mental Imaging

For the purposes of this book we will use the term Mental Imaging to include all forms of 'mind work', because essentially, by entering an altered state of awareness we are plugging into the creative side of our brain, and we can potentially gain access to the deepest part of our unconscious minds. Whether we use the power of myth to help us, positive affirmations to correct a flawed view of our 'self', visualisation exercises to change aspects of our lives, or mental exercises to aid our deep relaxation, we are working creatively with the mind and building images to replace the ones we would rather not have. We will discuss each of the mentioned parts of mental imaging separately, because each has a power and a use that is unique and useful under different sets of circumstances.

Relaxation and Affirmation

The original D. W. Ebrahim 'Sound of Calm' script makes very little use of the creative imagination. Instead the emphasis is on bodily sensations, particularly of course the sensation of deep muscle relaxation. After the initial induction via a flow of relaxation throughout the body, the state of awareness is further **deepened** by one of a number of possible **deepening techniques.**

Deepeners

All methods of deepening have certain things in common. There is usually downward movement, such as going down on a moving staircase to the count of ten. Each count is on an out breath. There are countless other images which will have the effect of deepening, such as for example going down in a lift or the too and fro motion of a pendulum, swinging in time to the breathing. Something completely different, and equally effective would be something like sitting on the bank of a river and tossing a leaf onto the water. Watch as it floats away, and with the next breath, toss another leaf onto the water, and so on. The possibilities are literally endless, so ones that "work for you" are obviously the best ones to use. Deepening techniques are particularly useful in self-induced altered states when for some reason we only manage to settle partially during the initial induction. Then it is essential to use the deepening technique. Other times when we seem to sink into the deepest state of relaxation almost immediately, we may choose to dispense with the deepening technique.

The late William Carr, a psychotherapist from Yorkshire, wrote one of the loveliest techniques I have ever found. It is full of wonderful words and imagery, and it does me good as therapist to read it, just as it has helped many of my clients too. His deepener takes me a long way back when he says that it's just as if you're lying down on an old fashioned feather bed, sinking deeper and deeper - then, "feather beds being what they are" ... my granny had one and I can still remember wrapping myself up in the luxurious feel of the feathers ... "you find yourself floating and sinking, round and round, down and down, just like a bird on outstretched, wonderful wings" ... (Appendix 2 on page 131 contains the full version of this text which is also on the CD).

In his preface, Hewitt, (1992) claims that the greatest benefits can be obtained from relaxation or meditation techniques if they are performed consistently twice daily, and each time for about 20 minutes. Research commissioned by the Transcendental Meditation Movement agrees with this. With regular practise it becomes easier to tell how "deep" we have gone, and therefore whether a deepening technique would be beneficial.

Many people report great difficulty with random thoughts that keep intruding and getting in the way of their most perfect relaxation. There is no easy solution to this. Some of us are more prone to 'busy minds', and if we explore that further, we will probably find that we tend to think a lot anyway, and probably worry about things. It may help to work towards focusing the mind on the *now* as much as we can - to experience every moment as fully as we are able.

Meditation techniques that make use of a mantra, or word repeated quietly in the mind, rely on the presence of the mantra to focus the mind sufficiently so as to avoid random thoughts intruding. Anyone who has practised these techniques however, will have found that the mantra alone is not enough. Thoughts still intrude. The instruction then is not to fight the thoughts, but as soon as there is awareness that the thoughts are present, to return the mind to mantra. In practise this can mean than an entire 20-minute session is spent following random thoughts! The only thing that can be said is that each time awareness of the run-away mind comes to the fore, this acts as reinforcement, and makes it slightly easier to remain focused on the mantra the next time. The other reason to adopt the practise of daily relaxation is that deep body relaxation occurs, and this in itself is a powerful weapon against stress and stress related illnesses. Sometimes, in the Western world, where we are in the age of the 'instant', from instant headache removal and instant indigestion soother, to instant mashed potato, we are not very kind to ourselves when it comes to practice, and feel that we should be able to do even difficult things instantly. Do remember that Eastern meditators will spend all their lives practising meditation, eventually being sent to practice in the market place, to be able to make their own peace amongst the hubbub!

Sister Brigid

A dear lady, a sister of an Anglican order attached to Chester Cathedral lived in the Retreat House. Their day was long, and seemed to me to be gruelling. Joint prayers started early enough, but before that each sister was expected to do two hours of private prayer. The sister said "I start my private prayer, and then I start to think of other things, all that I have to do in the day, what I'm going to make for breakfast, and dozens of other things. I clear my mind constantly. If I end up doing ten minutes of good quality prayer, I actually think I've done very well!"

Be kind to yourself, and recognise that you have done well if you manage the same as Sister Brigid who dedicated her life in this way.

Another option, which has been reported to be very useful by people who struggle to keep their 'mind on the job' so to speak, is the use of a pre-recorded cassette tape. Listening to a voice on a tape giving instructions makes it quite difficult to go off at a tangent with other thoughts.

The suggested 20 minutes twice daily has a powerful stress busting effect on both the body and the mind. In physical terms, stress causes an over-supply of adrenaline and other hormones, which prepare the body for action, called the 'flight and fight' mechanism. During our earlier evolution, humans had to escape danger – and quickly. If we came face to face with a sabre-toothed tiger, the huge surge of adrenaline would flood our body instantly, allowing for quick escape. The bowel would evacuate, shedding excess weight. Of course, most of the time action of the fight or flight sort for which the body is primed is inappropriate these days, in most situations, so the body remains flooded with stimulation. Over a period of time this level of over-stimulation becomes the base line. In other words we become 'used to' feeling the way we feel, but the various organs and endocrine glands become stressed by trying to cope with the constant 'red-alert' within the body, and the basis of disease is established.

In altered awareness deep relaxation the process is reversed, and the body is flooded with endorphins, which have a tranquillising effect on both body and mind. These beta-endorphins were isolated not that many years ago, as scientists worked on finding a cure for those who were addicted to opiates. To their great surprise, all humans were found to have their own built-in opiate supply that lies down the dorsal horn of the spinal column, waiting to be released and activated. Just imagine it. Not only is our own measured "feel-good factor" produced in exactly the right measure for ourselves, but our own pain-relief possibility too. All we would need was the training to activate what bio-chemically lies within us all. We can make ourselves feel better, which in itself is most welcome and valuable, but even more important, this process of deep relaxation also reduces the internal pressure on the organs and bodily systems - a time out from the normal red-alert condition. Over time the body becomes accustomed to this relaxation effect, and the red alert base line may be scaled down to yellow alert and finally to status normal. This is clearly of tremendous benefit to both mind and body, and has repercussions in areas such as work efficiency, state of mind and quality of relationships. In fact the 20 minute twice daily 'anti-stress routine' is the equivalent of getting a daily dose of natural tranquilliser, a tranquilliser made exactly to fit you by your own body, a tranquilliser that has only the positive side effect of enhanced general functioning. As previously mentioned, Jose Silva calls this state "alpha", the benefits of which can be further enhanced by the inclusion of any of a number of options, as follows:

Affirmations

We mentioned affirmations or techniques of ego strengthening in Part 1. These techniques can be used to good effect after a short period of deep relaxation. There are as many types of affirmation as there are needs for them. Ebrahim uses general suggestions in his 'Sound of Calm' script, first suggested by Hartland. He suggests feeling stronger and fitter, clearer of mind, better concentration, greater personal happiness and well-being, and so on. These suggestions or affirmations will have beneficial results for all people to the extent that we can all do with more of these things in our lives.

Jose Silva recommends that each time before coming out of 'alpha' that the affirmation of "feeling better than before", be used, and that the body be visualised in perfect health and the self in perfect happiness. More specific affirmations can also be used. Sarah, for example, entered therapy as part of a more general programme to help her cope with M.E. and osteo-arthritis in her knees. The specific symptom was that she found it difficult to walk due to heaviness in her legs, which got worse when she was tired. The affirmation she used at the end of each 20-minute session was 'the heaviness will leave my muscles, and my legs will feel light and energetic'.

An important point to remember when deciding on affirmations is to be sure to use words only in the positive. This is because in an altered state the 'interpreter' or 'programmer' that we spoke of earlier is not working quite so hard to make sense of our world. So the words we use enter our deepest awareness more or less unchanged, just as our early experiences were internalised without the benefit of our adult understanding. Stating things only in the positive means that we should say for instance, "I will be more understanding", rather than, "I will try not to misunderstand anymore". If we use the word "misunderstand", there is a danger of reinforcing our "misunderstanding" rather than our "understanding", which of course will result in us achieving the very opposite of our intention!

Stuart Wilde, already mentioned, recommends extended use of affirmations in daily life. He suggests a range of affirmations concerning the type of day we wish to have and the way we wish to feel in the morning. These can be written on a card and carried in the pocket, and repeated at regular intervals throughout the day. Louise Hay suggests a similar routine, with the addition of using specific affirmations when certain negative events occur in our lives. These techniques are all useful, because by changing our patterns of belief and thinking, we can change our lives, initially by how we respond to the situations that arise, and ultimately by changing the events themselves. Again each reader can decide and choose a system which fits in with the particular possibilities in their life.

Mind Control

Another useful device or technique that can be employed concerns the use of what psychotherapists would call 'post-hypnotic suggestion'. The use of affirmations while in a state of altered awareness does make use of post-hypnotic suggestion, or mind control. It is also possible to go quite a way beyond simple general affirmations when using altered states of awareness. Post hypnotic suggestion is a powerful tool in dealing with even serious health conditions, and this will be discussed at some length in the following section.

We have all had the experience of trying to remember a name or something else that seems to have disappeared from our minds completely. The harder we think about it and try to remember, the further it seems to slip away. Then suddenly, out of the blue the name or whatever pops off our tongue. Equally, we also hear stories of someone trying to find a solution to a particularly difficult problem. Suddenly in the middle of the night they wake up with a solution as clear as a bell in their minds. These examples are instances of the roundabout way the mind works. Memories that are not always immediately accessible come to the surface after a while, even after we have stopped thinking about them consciously, or, as in the second example, solutions appear as if by magic. In reality there is no magic about it. Just below the level of conscious awareness, a part of our minds has continued working on the problem we have set it, and usually continues until the problem is solved. Some people seem naturally better at this type of thinking than others, but do remember, practice makes perfect.

Techniques of altered awareness can use this natural process in a more focused way. Many guided mental imaging exercises make use of a character or figure to represent this process. Often the person is called a 'wise person' or 'helper' or 'healer', and the imaging exercise involves approaching this individual, usually via a complex or difficult route, and asking the questions that would offer the solutions or answers sought. This may seem a little far-fetched, and these techniques are often found in books or on tapes with a very mystical flavour that can put some people off, but the technique does not lose its effectiveness as a result of its mystical connections. The use of a person - wise person, healer, advisor or whatever simply plays into the tendency of the unconscious mind to work symbolically. Answers will probably not be forthcoming immediately, and may come in the middle of the night or at some other quiet time, and when they come, they will probably be accompanied by a sense of 'of course - why didn't I think of that before'. The method will work as well without personifying the function. Questions can be posed and solutions sought in an abstract way, and as with all things, with practise and regular use, mental muscle will be built up, and the technique will work faster and more efficiently.

There are many other common aspects to the control of the mind, or post hypnotic suggestion. Weight loss, stopping smoking, nail biting, insomnia, waking up on time, improved memory and many other behaviours are regularly changed effortlessly using this method. It is possible to achieve many of these things for ourselves via our own programming of our minds. All that is necessary is entry into the deepest state of relaxation and rest possible, using the methods outlined in the previous chapter, and then quite literally 'programming in' the desirable behaviour. For instance, if we are overweight because we eat between meals, we do not focus on the fact of being overweight. If we do this, our minds will hang onto the idea of overweight, and we will find it very difficult to shed the excessive weight we wish to shed. The phrase "losing" weight implies that something precious is going to go from us. Instead, by stating only in the positive, we use words such as full, no desire to eat between meals, and so on, and visualise ourselves at the weight we wish to be. Smokers need to talk about "stopping", not "giving up". You will notice the linguistic difference. We use the same technique to wake up in the morning at a specific time, or to stop smoking, or whatever it is we wish to change in our lives.

A word or two of caution: If we do not achieve the success we would like at the first, second or even the tenth attempt, it is easy to think that this does not work. Remember Albert Ellis, as previously quoted in his book *"Reason and Emotion in Psychotherapy"*. He says that if we work half as hard at getting better than we did in making ourselves ill in the first place, we will actually get better very quickly!

If the state of relaxation is not deep enough, then the programming will be proportionately less effective. As we saw with affirmations that are used during waking, they are repeated at regular intervals to be effective. The message goes deeper the more receptive we are, such as during a state of altered awareness. The closer to normal waking awareness we are, the more like an affirmation and the less like a post-hypnotic suggestion our image or words will be. Suggestibility exists along a continuum. At one end frequent repetition breaks down resistance to a new idea, and at the other deep altered awareness makes it possible for an idea to be inserted deeply and effectively with relatively less attempts. The only way to achieve a desired goal is to continue working at it until we get there. Sometimes the only encouragement available is the knowledge that others before have done what we are trying to do.

A further caution is that sometimes things like nail biting, being over weight or smoking are the result of other, deeper issues. Fortunately our awareness of this fact grows the more time we spend with ourselves, and time spent in relaxation qualifies not only in terms of quantity but also of quality. If we choose to programme ourselves to lose weight, we may well lose the weight we want to lose, but the feelings that the extra weight literally "held down" will then surface, and we will need to deal with them.

Sometimes, in cases like these it is a good idea to seek out a qualified therapist to help us get a perspective on what is happening inside of us. One thing is certain, and if we are honest we will be able to admit this at some level, and that is if we use these techniques, things will begin to change in our lives. The change will be for the better, if we can allow it to proceed, but the process of change is not always comfortable or easy, so there may be a little bit of a bumpy ride for a while.

One more thing deserves mention. This is something that is still on the fringes of popular thinking, and to date has not featured much in our practise of psychotherapy, except where it has formed part of the belief system of individual clients. José Silva, in his commercially available training called 'The Silva Mind Control Method', which in reality is a formalised and well packaged (and therefore accessible) form of self hypnosis, has made a conceptual leap which has not been followed by many to date. Silva believes that not only is it possible to access these hidden places within ourselves, but by entering 'alpha' it is possible to connect with certain unconscious functions in other people. The way he says it is that the unconscious of one can speak with the unconscious of another. This is not the same as reading someone's mind, or trespassing in the private reaches of another person's world. An example he uses is that if someone else mislays something, it is possible to find it by entering 'alpha' ourselves, and then asking the unconscious of the other person where they put the object. Unlikely as this may sound, some impressive results have been obtained using these techniques, and some of the hush-hush research that has been conducted into the use of mind surveillance prior to the end of the cold war does raise interesting questions. The best I can suggest is that if this area interests anyone, that it be pursued on a personal level. The method Silva suggests is the same as the one I've outlined. Enter the deepest levels of alpha, and then simply try it out. My personal view and experience is that we have not yet discovered the limits of mind capability, so the best course is open-mindedness.

Healing

There are impressive stories of how people have cured or helped even severe physical illness using methods of mental imaging. Stress and other states of mental anguish have also found relief through the use of visualisation. Again there are countless specific scripts of visualisations that can be used to great effect. I must state one caution though. The use of these mental techniques is just that – using mental techniques, of the order of mental imaging as we discussed in Part 1. The effect that they have is similar to an athlete using mental imaging to improve his skill. Although, as I have said, such work has the effect of widening the neural pathways in the brain, which does lead to better performance, *only* using mental imaging and never practising in reality is not enough to produce an athlete of any standard. Similarly, these healing techniques should not be used *instead of* sensible medical care. They should be used together with medical care, especially for serious conditions. The use of mental techniques cannot have a negative effect on medical conditions, so they can be used safely alongside more conventional medical, herbal, homeopathic or other forms of treatment.

Gloria

Gloria had suffered from severe eczema for many years. She came to therapy not so much to deal with the eczema as to learn techniques of relaxation. She found the 'Sound of Calm' very useful and returned after the first week well pleased with herself for having managed two twenty-minute sessions each day. In the second week the therapist introduced another component to the exercise. She asked Gloria to imagine herself naked in her bedroom, and to imagine a small brush in her hand. She was then asked to begin to brush her skin gently, starting with her torso and working towards her hands and her feet. As she brushed, she was to imagine her eczema turning dry and flaky and falling off in little clouds of flakes with each brush stroke. She was to imagine her skin pink and healthy where the brush had passed. When she had finished she was to look at herself in the mirror and see her skin in perfect health. The following week Gloria returned beaming. She lifted the sleeves of her shirt to reveal two or three small patches of eczema where her entire limb had been covered before.

Clearly not in all cases are reactions as speedy and as dramatic as with Gloria, but nevertheless the positive results achieved in therapeutic practise leave no doubt in my mind that these techniques of healing work, and work well. There are three different scripts, which between them I have found, give the basis for treating most conditions:

The Magic Garden

This is suitable for use when we feel that things are a burden and getting on top of us. It is effective in terms of physical, mental and emotional conditions. The script, used at Centre Training International School of Hypnotherapy and Psychotherapy, and devised by myself, is as follows. The script as it stands is suitable for reading onto a tape for personal use, or read it through a few times, then imagine the sequence of events. (Appendix 3 which is on page 159 contains the full version of this text which is also on the CD at the back of the book).

Picture a garden in your mind's eye. Make it an English Country Garden, with a high wall right around the end, trees and creepers growing over the wall, tall flowers in front of it, smaller flowers in front of that and smaller flowers still in front of that, right down to tiny flowers at your feet, all packed so closely together that you can hardly see any soil. Feel the warmth of the sun on your head and on your back and smell the sweet scent of flowers all about, the sun shinning, the sky as blue as blue can be, and all around you an atmosphere of peace, and calm and tranquillity.

There are insects too. Little buzzing things, big fat bees, pretty butterflies, and if you are very lucky, maybe a dragonfly, translucent wings and beautiful iridescent body. There are birds twittering about the place, with their coloured plumage and sweet songs; lawns, little paths, flowering shrubs, and somewhere, water tinkling about the place....

Go down to the bottom of the garden where the tall trees are. Tied to the tree with a big stout rope is a big balloon filled with lighter than air gas and swinging from the bottom of it, a large empty box, hovering 4 or 6 inches above the ground. It's a very special box. It can contain things that you want rid of. Look around inside yourself and see if there's anything inside you'd be better off without. When you find something, take it and push it into the box.

When you've done that, untie the big stout rope that holds down the balloon. The balloon will lift that box up, lighter and lighter, higher and higher. Higher and higher until it gets to the top of the tallest tree. Lighter and lighter and higher and higher, until it is as small as the nail on your little finger. Lighter and lighter and higher and higher until it disappears in a dot and the sky is clear. Eventually, the balloon will burn up in the atmosphere, and whatever you've put into the box will burn up too, and will be transformed into light.

Turn back to the garden now, and find yourself somewhere pleasant and peaceful to be - just sit, or lie, and fill up the space inside yourself, the space that you've just made by putting things into the box.

The visualisation of the garden can be expanded for other purposes as well, and most people find the idea of a safe, walled garden very appealing, and a place to which they can retreat in times of stress and discomfort. One client described her garden as a 'safety net' in her uncertain life. If you don't like gardens, choose a place that you do like, and where you feel safe, perhaps a beach, or a meadow. Details such as where the balloon is tied can be fitted in appropriately.

Another useful technique that has been used most effectively is to enter the garden and follow the sound of water, till a healing pool, or waterfall is reached. The exercise could then proceed along the lines of entering the pool and / or standing under the waterfall, and allowing the water to wash through the body, pouring through the skin and washing and healing parts which are diseased or ill. It is useful here to visualise the organs actually bathed in the healing water, and growing pinker and healthier as the water washes over them. The water can also be used to wash away pain. Powerful jets of water have been used effectively in cases of arthritis and other similar conditions. By visualising these jets of healing water washing through the joints and clearing away the debris deposited there, great benefit has been found. These are exercises that need to be repeated frequently.

Olive

Olive, aged 7, was brought by her mother. She had been diagnosed with an incurable condition. She had become listless. Her tendons had tightened, drawing her legs in towards her body, as one would expect the back legs of a frog to be. Her feet, too, had drawn inwards like clubs, with the outside of the foot pointed downwards. She was totally unable to walk. As well as that, her legs were ulcerated from top to bottom. Olive entered the garden. She unloaded one thing into the box, and chose never to disclose to me or to her parents what that was. The tinkling water, I suggested was a fountain, and she imagined peeling off her clothes and getting in, feeling the water like silk over her skin - then it trickling through the top of her head, cleansing and refreshing her inside and out, trickling out of the ends of her feet, rather grubbier than when it had gone in, for all the cleansing it had been doing.

Just before her appointment with me, Olive had been to the hospital to be measured for a pair of boots that would help her feet fit flatly on to the floor. She would never wear those boots, which took a month or so to make. Miraculously, after a week, when Olive returned, all the ulcers had gone. She had cleansed herself. Her mother reported that she was "brighter". Over the next few weeks, her legs started to straighten, and she became more outgoing. Her little brother had a push-around trolley filled with wooden bricks. Her father had put a sitting flat piece on it, and Olive was scooting up and down the road with the other children. The last time I saw her, she said to me "I can hop 32 times!" She was very thrilled with herself. She was wonderfully courageous, and had no limits in her mind as to what the possibilities were for her.

Talking about limits, please look at the exercise below. This exercise might be familiar to you – if you have not met it before please give it a whirl. Even if you have met it, do you remember the principle? There are lots of people who cannot do it.

EXERCISE 15

SELF LIMITATION / EXPANSION
Give yourself 5 minutes for this exercise

1.   Join together the nine dots with four straight lines.

2.   You must not double back on yourself.

3.   You must not lift the pen off the paper.


```
*           *           *



*           *           *



*           *           *
```

The solution to this exercise is shown at Appendix 6.

Did you get the point of putting in this exercise? How many of us restrict ourselves to the visible parameters – the parameters that have, perhaps, been given us by another. Even if this exercise is familiar, you may well have got the point of limitation at some stage of your life that this exercise attempts to highlight for you.

The Healing Room

A healing technique borrowed and adapted from Betty Shine's 'Mind Medicine Room' (*Mind to Mind* 1990 p 243) concerns the creation of a mental Healing Room. It may be comfortable to have this room in a special house in the walled garden. An important point to remember is that both the garden and whatever is in it are totally personal, and should be created according to our inner images and wishes. Inside the house, at the end of a passage, in Betty Shine's version, or in a secret room, hidden behind a panel in the huge walk-in fireplace lies a special, healing room.

This room should be mentally constructed according to the needs of the individual. In the centre of the room can be a chair or a bed, and around the walls can be shelves containing jars and bottles of every shape and size. In these bottles and jars are everything necessary to heal any condition we may have, mental, emotional or physical. In the room also can be someone else - the healer I suggested earlier. This person can be anyone at all, but should be described as someone who knows us better than ourselves, and who has all the knowledge and information that will enable them to help us, should we so wish. Betty Shine recommends that we label the jars ourselves over time, as we enter this room and that once we have labelled the jar, it will automatically contain all we need to heal us. (Appendix 4 contains the full version of this script).

One version of the visualisation exercise involves lying on the bed/sitting in the chair and asking our helper to do what is necessary to heal us. This may involve the use of something from a bottle or jar, or warmth or light. At the end of the treatment, our helper may give us a gift - or we may take from the room a jar or bottle of whatever was used on us, for regular use while away from the room. Before we leave, we need to understand quite clearly that we have the power and the ability to visit this room at any time we need to do so.

Sarah

We have already met Sarah. She came to therapy suffering with osteo-arthritis and M.E. She was under doctor's treatment for her condition, but was not happy taking so many drugs and wished to stop medical treatment. She and I agreed to work with her on condition that she did not stop medication without her doctor's consent. Her knees were very swollen and painful, and her legs seemed so heavy at times that she found it almost impossible to go upstairs to bed. She didn't feel that her drugs were having any effect, except perhaps in terms of pain relief.

Sarah was delighted to go into the healing room, and her helper applied a liberal quantity of ointment to her knees. Her helper also gave her a jar of this ointment to take out of the room, to be applied each morning and each evening. She did this regularly each day during her period of relaxation. Combined with the positive affirmations concerning a new lightness in her legs, Sarah began to find her energy levels increasing, and the swelling and pain in her knees decreasing. Equipped with the tools for her own healing, she worked diligently every day; till she felt so much better that she was able to speak to her doctor about decreasing her medication.

The Three Dimensional Storage System

The final technique I would like to put forward is a version of one suggested by Syer and Connolly (1984) for use with sports people to help them put aside distractions that may get in the way of their performance. I have found it of wider use, for dealing with the many different types of things people find cluttering their minds, distracting them from matters that need their immediate attention. It is a technique of particular value to busy people, or people burdened by worries or concerns.

The version I use is to enter our house in our walled garden, (again adapt this according the where your 'special place is) and to find in it a large, sunny room. In the corner of the room you have a beautiful desk, and a large, comfortable swivel chair. Behind the desk are shelves, some of them filled with books and on others ornaments and small boxes. We sit at the desk, and find in front of us a pile of white paper, and beside that a pen.

Looking inside, you select something that you wish to put aside for the moment, and using the pen, represent this 'something' somehow on the paper. You fold the paper and put it to one side, and repeat the process, until you no longer have anything we wish to put aside. Putting down the pen, you swivel around on your chair and take from the shelf a beautifully made box with a lid. Swivel back, open the box and place inside it the papers on which you have written. Close the box, turn back to the shelf and replace the box. As you do so, you are aware that this is only temporary storage, and make a contract with yourself to return to the box and deal with whatever you have put aside.

The exercise ends by leaving the room, going back into the garden, and just like with the 'Magic Garden' exercise, finding a pleasant place to sit or lie, and fill up the space you have made inside with peace, tranquillity and deep rest. (Appendix 5 on page 163 contains the full version of the text which is also spoken for you on the CD).

These three primary visualisation exercises have almost limitless possibilities for change and adaptation to individual needs. There are also hundreds of other possibilities, but as with everything, sometimes too much choice is as bad as no choice at all. Distilling down to these three ensures that a comfortable and manageable balance is struck.

Performance Enhancement

By combining some of the techniques given above, it is possible to influence our performance in many aspects of life.   Performance enhancement is not only useful for professional sports people, it has uses that extend way beyond this - from improving performance during exams, to driving, to stage work, to in fact anything that we find ourselves doing on a daily basis. It can be used in a purely physical sense or for non-physical activities. Regular visualisation of favourable outcomes can do wonders for those who suffer from stage fright, or lack confidence before public speaking. Visualisation of positive or desirable outcomes can also be useful in a business context, where for example a sales person may visualise a stream of customers coming towards them, or a negotiator may visualise closing the deal.

Silva suggests the creation of a mental screen for this purpose. He suggests that when we reach 'alpha' a room be created, much in the same way that the healing room is created in the mind's eye. Imagine a large screen in this room, like a TV screen, and project images of the self onto the screen, performing the desired activity perfectly.   This is an important aspect of Positive Mental Attitude, but goes further, in that it instigates the process of neural development, necessary for the easy execution of any action.

It will be easy, with the information contained in these pages, to customise performance enhancement scripts for every conceivable situation. The key lies in regular practise. The greatest effect is achieved when we reach the point where we realise that we hold within ourselves the power to be whatever we choose, and that we have the skill and ability to access this power to change. This deceptively simple realisation is one that cannot fail to have a positive effect once we allow it into our consciousness.

Throughout this section we have been working at knowing ourselves better, and working out how to deal with different stimuli. The exercise following is designed to help you with this as your awareness grows about your body – how it feels, and where you feel your feelings.

EXERCISE 16

BECOMING AWARE OF OUR FEELINGS.
This could take about 30 minutes

1. Get ready to make a list.

2. Think of as many "feeling" words as you can.

3. Think of the physical sensations associated with these emotions:

    E.g. When I feel worried I have a tight, sick feeling in my stomach.

    E.g. When I feel fed up I feel flushed in my face and have a tight feeling in my head.

4. When, and in what situations do you feel these emotions?

    E.g. I get worried when the boss is in a "mood".

    E.g. I feel fed up when I get told what to do all the time.

It is interesting to become aware of feelings in this way. Having become aware it is possible to take the exercise a stage further by working out where you feel something when in some way thwarted from one of your needs being met.

EXERCISE 17

HOW YOU FEEL WHEN YOUR NEEDS ARE NOT BEING MET
This could take about 30 minutes

1.   Take a pen and paper to write a list once more.

2.   Take a minute or two to identify two feelings you commonly
experience when someone is doing something you don't like.

Explore those feelings, the postures associated with them and note: -

Where in my body do I feel them?

What position is associated with that feeling?

What happens if I change my position when I'm feeling like that?
What is it that triggers that feeling?

What other feelings lie hidden underneath that feeling?

As well as giving us the obvious benefit of knowledge of ourselves, exploring feelings in this way opens up the possibility of doing things differently, giving us more options as to how we tackle things in the future.

9

Bridging the Gap - Communication

The ideas and techniques found in the **Peace of Mind** programme have been borrowed from numerous sources. That is because I do not believe that human behaviour can be circumscribed by any single set of ideas or theories. Nor do I believe that any one set of techniques is useful for all people, because we all have our own unique frame of reference and set of experiences. The NLP or Neuro-Linguistic Programming model is one such system. This chapter is not an attempt to explain or explore all the tenets of NLP. On the contrary, I would like to present a series of techniques gleaned from NLP which I have found useful both in my personal quest for **Peace of Mind** and in the lives of my clients. I have found that these techniques can help us to understand ourselves and to cope with our lives more creatively, and in the context of this book they form part of the process of shifting our attention towards our relationships with others.

NLP - Basic Definition

NLP is a blend of cognitive and behavioural science, and was devised by linguist Dr. John Grinder and computer scientist and Gestalt therapist Dr. Richard Bandler. In essence, a knowledge of the principles of NLP brings to our awareness an understanding and an appreciation of the unconscious principles surrounding the process of communication. It includes both verbal and non-verbal communication. In its entirety it offers an explanation of how the brain works, of how and often why language is produced, and how we use communication to get what we want from others.

The Map Versus the Territory

The only way we can receive information from our world and about our world is via our senses, and sadly these can be quite unreliable at times, due to many reasons. Consequently the picture of the world which we hold inside ourselves does not necessarily represent an accurate reflection of the world as it is objectively, out there. This means that the way we see the world can be very different to the way someone else sees the world. In NLP terms a differentiation is made between the "map", or an individual representation and the "territory", the (supposed) objective reality. Just as with geographical maps, our internal map is useful for our particular purpose. That's fine for us individually, but when it comes to communicating with someone who has a different map, we may find ourselves becoming a little unstuck! It can be a bit like explaining how to go by road from point A to point B to someone who has a detailed topographical map of the area! The same can and does happen to us each day in our communications with others.

Representational Systems

Our internal representational system or 'rep' system can be compared to a map. Just as a geographical map is made from observation, measurement and experience, so an internal rep system is constructed from past experience. At any moment in time we have a number of sensory experiences available to us. Many of these we don't need, so depending on the situation, we learn which messages to respond to, and which to ignore. We delete some of the information, we may distort other information, and in this way we build up a conscious picture of the way the world appears to us. From the array of information available, we may find that what we see is most useful, or what we hear, or we may find the way we feel to be the most useful information. Over time we come to rely more and more on a particular way of gathering information. If we favour visual information, for example, we will probably ignore at least some of the sounds we can hear at the time, or we may pay less attention to how we feel. This also represents the way we remember an event - in terms of the information we have about it. NLP teaches that people fall into one of a combination of categories based on which of their senses they use the most.

As language is a representation of our world, the words we use to describe it can be an indicator of our rep system. So if we are **visual** we tend to *see* what someone means or things will *look* or *appear* this way or that. If we are **auditory** we may *hear* things loud and clear, things will *click* into place, or *ring* bells for us. If we are **kinaesthetic** we will *get in touch with* someone or something, have a *sense* of something or find that things *fit* nicely. Although we do gather information via taste and smell, it is less common for these senses to be dominant, although many of us will remember a situation that *left a bad taste in our mouth,* or when something *smelt fishy*!

A simple exercise will give you a good idea of your own rep system.

EXERCISE 18

PREDICATE WORDS
(This should take you 10-15 minutes)

1. Write down in story form, what you did this morning from the time you opened your eyes.

2. Stop when you've filled about half a page, and divide the rest of the page into four columns, under the headings of, Visual, Auditory, Kinaesthetic, Un-specified.

3. Then go through the passage and classify the words you used in terms of the sense they relate to.

4. Visual words will be any visually descriptive adjectives, such as "look", "see" and other words relating to vision.

5. Auditory words will cover aspects of sound, from "crunch", "hoot" and "tweet" to words describing sound in terms of volume, tone, pitch, timbre and so on.

6. Kinaesthetic words relate to inner feelings as well as to the sense of touch, temperature, texture and also to movement. So here we have "slip into", "turn around", "soft", "rough", "keep abreast of", and so on.

7. Unspecified words and phrases are those such as "process", "make sense of", "think", "consider". You may find that one of your lists is longer than the others. If so, you may have identified your rep system. Try to become aware of the words that you use in everyday language until you are sure. It may be that your words are divided evenly into the different categories, or that two are stronger than the other.

Some examples of the types of words that you may have identified in the above exercise and the categories that they fall into are:

VISUAL	AUDITORY	KINAESTHETIC	UN-SPECIFIED
See	Hear	Feel	Sense
Look	Listen	Touch	Experience
View	Sound(s)	Grasp	Understand
Appear	Harmonise	Get hold of	Think
Show	Tune in	Slip through	Learn
Dawn	Be all ears	Catch on	Process
Reveal	Rings a bell	Tap into	Decide
Envision	Silence	Make contact	Motivate
Image	Be heard	Throw out	Consider
Picture	Resonate	Turn around	Change
Clear	Deaf	Hard	Perceive
Foggy	Talk	Concrete	Distinct
Focused	Speak	Scrape	Conceive
Hazy	Whine	Solid	Be conscious
Sparkling	Chime	Cemented	Know
Flash	Chatter	Soft	Wonder
Frame	Call	Keep abreast of	Realise
Vague	Tell	Fuzzy	Convince
Watch	Noise	Stiff	Plan
Colourful	Echo	Firm	Create
Sight	Sing	Cool	Identify
Dim	Volume	Flowing	Motivate

Whatever the outcome of Exercise 18 for you, it should have provided some valuable information to you. Imagine what might happen when a person who is visual tries communicating with someone who is kinaesthetic? A useful example of this is provided by Steve Lankton, who describes a client - therapist conversation in his book "Practical Magic" (1980, p.19):

"The following example, perhaps familiar to you, demonstrates how two well-intentioned people fail to make contact on the first, and therefore most vital, step of communication.

*Client: "I'm so **hurt**". My husband left and I **feel** so helpless … so alone. I've never **felt** so much **pain**, do you know what I mean?"*

*Therapist: "let me **see** if I understand this; I want to be **clear** on the source of your pain. Would you **focus** in and get a **picture** of your pain and we'll see if that tells us how to deal with it".*

*Client: (pause) "I just tried to get **hold** of a picture but I just **feel** worse. I don't **feel** like you're in **touch** with my difficulty".*

The therapist may conclude that the client is "resistant" and the client already considers the therapist insensitive.   Now this is a slight exaggeration, but not much."

It is like the two different maps I described earlier.   If communication is to be effective, we have somehow to 'get inside' the world of the other person. If we can see the world through his or her eyes, even for a few moments, we are in a better position to bridge the gap between us. "How?" you may ask. Read on.

Modelling - the NLP Methodology

NLP started out as a system of modelling. The point of interest was the way some people managed to get on in life and make a success of what they did, while others consistently struggled and failed.   The hypothesis was that if someone who was usually not successful began to do the things that a successful person did, then they too would become successful.   Bandler and Grinder found that in order to do this, it was necessary to reproduce what the other person did inside their head - to use the language they used, and to use the internal filters and 'rep' system that they used.   This led to the many and varied techniques of NLP - techniques which were then found to be valuable in a wider context.

In terms of communicating with someone who functions from a different rep system to your own, if you *modelled* their method of communication, they would be able to understand you more easily. To do this effectively takes a bit of practise. First of all you need to become aware of how you communicate, as well as how they communicate. Then you have to change your inner system to match theirs'. If you are visual, and have never really thought about it, you would first need to exercise your observational muscles, just as you would exercise your physical muscles.   This involves conscious observation rather than automatic observation. Visual people will need to pay careful attention to the way the world smells, feels, tastes and sounds. As a visual person, be aware of the way you feel inside - what does it feel like when you go to a crowded shopping centre, or to a quiet beach. Where in your body do you feel - is it a sensation, or just a sense of something? Perhaps you can close your eyes sometimes, so that you can experience your world in a different way. With practice it will become easier both to identify the way other people experience the world, and to change the way you process your information to match the way they process theirs.

The other thing to pay attention to is the use of language. Try out different words - if you normally say *I see,* try saying *I hear what you say,* or *that fits.* Language is both powerful and subtle. By practising the use of other words, you make subtle shifts in your internal processing which makes matching someone else all the easier.

Building Rapport

Changing your rep system to match that of someone else is one of the ways of building rapport. Rapport is the word used to indicate the extent to which two people are on the same wavelength. There are many reasons why we would want to get on someone else's wavelength. Sales training has made extensive use of NLP techniques, because the theory is that if someone feels heard and understood, it makes them more willing to accept what you say - and of course, in the end to buy your product. However, good rapport has a much wider value than that.

As a little exercise, think about an occasion when you said something and it seemed as if the person or people you were talking to didn't hear or understand what you were saying.

EXERCISE 19

NOT BEING UNDERSTOOD
(This should take about 5 minutes)

1.   Think back to a time or times in the past, if possible from childhood or teens, when you said something, and it seemed as if the person or people you were talking to didn't hear or understand what you were talking about.

2.   How did you feel?

It may have been way back in childhood, or it may have been last week, when you were asked a question and your reply was ignored. Remembering how that felt, imagine trying to get something across to someone - a partner, a child, a boss, a bank manager or a new date - and they feel the same way that you did. It would be impossible for them to hear your message, because they would be too busy reeling at the shock of the experience, or protecting themselves against further harm.   In whatever context, knowing how to establish rapport, or to build a relationship is a valuable skill, because successful interaction as a human being depends on it.

When looking at (or getting a sense of!) rapport, it is useful to consider all possible aspects of communication. Allan Pease, in his book *Body Language*, (1981, p.9) quotes the findings of research done by Albert Mehrabian back in 1969.   Mehrabian found that of our total communication, only 7% are the words we use. We transmit 38% of our message in the tone of our voice and a massive 55% in the attitude and posture of our body.   If this is true, and other research also quoted by Pease indicates that it is, then it makes sense to consider ways of working on *how* we say things as well as on *what* we say if we want to establish rapport with someone.

Pacing

Pacing is the term used to describe the whole range of behaviours that are designed to set the other person at ease - to build rapport with them. What pacing someone else's behaviour does is to send a subtle message to them which says, "Let us go at your pace for a while - let us be in your world together, let us talk the same language, and let me accept you completely, no matter how different we are".

Superficially the process of matching the behaviour of someone else may seem bizarre - or even rude, but it must be remembered that most of the things we do with our body are done without thinking, and without even knowing we do them. Anyone who has had the experience of watching themselves on a video will appreciate this - so as long as what we do remains below the conscious threshold of the other person, it will be recognised unconsciously by them.   The late Dr. Milton Erickson MD of Phoenix, Arizona, put this beautifully when he said that mirroring the (physical) behaviour of another person has the effect of "paying the unconscious mind a gracious compliment".   Essentially we are saying 'I see and recognise you - what you do has value - see, I do it too!'

Mirroring and Matching

We mirror the behaviour of someone when we do what they do, but to the opposite side, so that we form a mirror image of them. If they sit with the left leg crossed over the right leg, and we sit with our right leg crossed over their left leg, we present a mirror to them. We match them if we do the same as they do, and on the same side. Most of us use a mirror every day to see ourselves. And some of us may have had the experience - especially with a child - when they mirror what we do, or echo the exact words or phrases we use and this gives us the opportunity to re-evaluate our behaviour. There are many tales of less than savoury phrases coming out of the mouths of babes, forcing parents to realise that they themselves use those words! Mirroring may have this effect, but on an unconscious level. By the same logic, matching sends a message that says 'I'm with you'.

EXERCISE 20

MATCHING / MISMATCHING
Please find a friend who will give you 15 minutes

Please do the exercise below, carefully! See how powerful it is to deliberately mismatch someone. You may well find this upsetting to do as well as to be on the receiving end of!

1. Find a partner who you feel comfortable with.
2. Tell your partner in advance what this exercise is going to consist of.
3. Each person is to take about seven minutes to share with the other something they feel strongly about. For example, a current dilemma or issue, their favourite way to relax, something they remember lovingly from their childhood.
4. For two minutes partners should try to be UNHELPFUL by mismatching, then,
5. Partners should listen silently - say nothing at all and really concentrate on communicating the attitudes of ACCEPTING, CARING, UNDERSTANDING and TRUSTING, making their best efforts to let the speaker know that they care about what they are saying.
6. Swap round after seven minutes.
7. Give each other feedback as to how you felt during this exercise.

In the Field

Dr. Don Ebrahim, one of my old teachers, told an interesting story about his practice time on his NLP Practitioner Training Course. The *students were sent out to 'work in the field' experimenting with mirroring and matching. He went into a busy, crowded pub to order a drink. The bar was four deep. It needs to be said at this point that Don, though extremely English, is of South African extraction from an African mother and an Indian father. As well as that, for a man he is quite small at about 5 foot 3 inches.*

Just imagine this added dimension of colour and height, which unfortunately, in some parts of the world, might have worked against him in the aforementioned scenario of a crowded pub. Don spotted a busy barman acting rather strangely shrugging his shoulders up and down quite regularly whilst serving drinks.

Putting his new-found skills to the test, Don mirrored him and started to shrug also. Don was still three back in the queue, when the barman had finished serving his previous customer when he spoke over two shoulders to Don – "Yes sir. What can I get you?"

Breathing patterns are another, subtle way of doing this. If we breathe at the same pace as the person we are with - we establish quite a powerful bond with them. Fast panting breaths are typical in situations of difficulty or distress.

It is no accident that antenatal classes teach the coach to breathe and to pant with the woman giving birth. If we pace our breathing with someone who is distressed for a little while, and then gradually begin to breathe more slowly and more naturally, we subtly lead them towards a more relaxed state. We can also lead in the same way to help someone feel more relaxed and at ease by matching the way they sit, and then after a little while begin to relax ourselves. Chances are the other person will follow, and their body will communicate a greater openness. If someone doesn't follow our lead, all we do is go back to matching him or her for a little while, then lead again. If we repeat this pattern a few times, they will follow.

It is also not necessary to mimic behaviour or posture completely. If someone crosses his or her legs at the knee, for instance, we can cross ours at the ankle. The message still gets through to the subconscious mind.

All this may sound rather far-fetched. As with everything else in this book, all that I ask from the reader is an open mind, and all that I offer is my experience. Try it out. You can have a lot of fun matching the behaviour of the people around you - and see whether it has any effect. Personal experience is the only real way to learn.

State Maintenance

Knowing how we feel and how we experience our world in any given moment is very important. If we know how we feel, we can also distinguish between our feelings and the feelings and expectations that other people project onto us which we accept or 'take on'. Guilt is a classic example of the way we take on things from other people. If we do something we wished we hadn't, that is one thing, and we can deal with that in time, learning from our experience, but most of the guilt we carry around with us is because we didn't act or think or feel the way someone else wanted us to. That does not belong to us - it belongs to them. We have looked at this under 'whose problem' in Part 1, but reiterate it here in terms of the importance of being aware of our own inner state. NLP identifies a *resourceful state* as a comfortable state that is appropriate to the circumstances in which we find ourselves.

This may sound simpler than it is. We have discussed how we can become accustomed to a constant rate of over-stress, and how our system can begin to consider a state of 'red alert' to be the norm. The longer such a state persists, the easier it becomes to forget that there is any other possibility, leading us to accept that this is literally as good as it gets. This is only one example of the way an inappropriate state can be confused with a resourceful state. Awareness of our inner state is therefore of prime importance. NLP says quite simply that if a state does not serve us then we should change it. This too sounds easier than it is, but careful exploration leads us to see that quite often we accept the way things are simply because we do not believe in our ability to make the necessary changes. This is a flaw in thinking, and when recognised, can be corrected.

So, once we have recognised an uncomfortable state, what can we do to change it?

Anchoring

This involves focusing the attention on physical conditions or circumstances that were present during periods of resourceful mind states. The following example illustrates the point:

While living and working in a beautiful rural setting in Wales, Sam loved to gaze out over the hills at sunset and watch everything turn an unbelievable shade of gold with red foxes walking through the bracken. The sights always filled him with delight and awe, and gave him the strength to face whatever came his way. As he stood in the kitchen and looked out, he often hugged himself in delight, squeezing his upper arms with his opposite hands. Years later he found that performing the same action - i.e. squeezing his upper arm with his opposite hand would evoke vivid memories of the scene that delighted him in Wales. The feel-good experience he had while watching the sunset was instantly re-created each time. It is almost as if the memory of the pleasant event had imprinted itself in his upper arms. This process can be explained in terms of the association of the squeezed upper arm with the pleasant memory.

Massage therapists frequently experience a negative aspect of this phenomenon. They often report that clients want to discuss things that come up as a result of being massaged. This is because of the anchoring of painful experiences in certain parts of the body. We can use this technique of anchoring to put ourselves into a resourceful state, either by programming a trigger for a resourceful state into certain parts of the body and then accessing them as we need them, or by using existing positive anchor points.

In a more general sense, anchoring can be seen as an exercise in grounding. By becoming aware of our physical circumstances we can use body awareness to change the way we think about the circumstance which we find uncomfortable. Often emotional distress is located in one part of the body, and by focusing on a different part of the body we can change the level of distress. It is useful to programme a positive anchor for use in specific circumstances, such as for instance to help deal with stage fright.

Stage Fright

The most unexpected people can suffer from the most unexpected things. One of our therapists had an unannounced caller whilst in practice in Liverpool. It suffices to say that he was a famous comedian from the city. He had to appear on the Royal Command Variety Show and was nervous to appear in front of the Queen.

Very willing to learn, he worked on some techniques and, after a few visits, was asked to future-pace himself (see forward as to what he would look like on the night of the performance). 'Magnificent', he said, bringing, if you will, that visualised picture of the future back to the present to be used as a resource for himself.

Using his anchoring, Sound of Calm and other things, he coped admirably, and, at the performance, no one would have known that he had ever had a nervous impulse in his body!

Change in Breathing

We have seen how a change in breathing rhythm affects our state of awareness. By altering the focus of our awareness, we can change the intensity of an experience, and thereby move towards a more resourceful state. On a simple physiological level, a change in the blood gas composition affects the balance of our emotions.

Change in Posture

Changing posture, or moving about, changes our level of energy, which in turn changes the way we feel. So often, when we're feeling down, the eyes drop and the shoulders droop. We hunch ourselves up and feel bad. It is no accident that our distant forefathers and the Jewish religion left us the words of Psalm 121. It says, "I will lift up mine eyes unto the hills from whence cometh my help". Religion often uses this; most help comes from somewhere above. No matter what we believe, just looking up, raising our eyes and shoulders does help us to feel better. The NLP model rather hogged the fact that to look up (moving our eyes into the place which allowed our visual accessing to be most dominant for most people) made us feel better, but actually, the empirical evidence has been there for over two thousand years.

Know Desired Outcome

If we know how we would like to feel, it is easier to change our mental state. Turn your desired outcome into a simple statement, remembering to state it in the positive.

Changing Sub-modalities

Modalities or sensory modalities is the NLP way of referring to our senses, and sub-modalities are the smaller classes of classification within one of the senses, used to categorise experience. For example, having the sense of a great weight on our shoulders, or being weighed down by a particular problem is the way the problem is processed by our kinaesthetic sense. Mentally we know the details of our problem, and may even be busy solving it, but it has an effect on the way we *feel,* and that effect is of a great weight. We may feel happy, and describe it as a silver stream of bubbles flowing through our body. This would be a more visual element of a kinaesthetic experience.

When we change sub-modalities, we change the nature of this experience, the reasoning being that the sensory experience has an influence on the situation. In the example of the problem being a great weight - removing the weight will not necessarily solve the problem, but once the weight is removed, we will feel differently about the situation, and taking the metaphor even further - once the weight is removed, we will be able to look up - and perhaps find a solution to what seemed insoluble before.

The way to do this is best described by an example.

Roy

Roy is a thirteen-year-old youth from an economically needy inner city school. I was called in by his school. He was showing behavioural difficulties, finding it difficult to concentrate, and seemed to have outbursts of anger, with all the disruptions to his classroom situation that you may imagine. He was very open. After a couple of sessions of getting to know him, I asked about his anger, in terms of colour, shape, texture, density and so on, he described it as a heavy black steel ball the size of a football over the front of his head. It didn't sound very comfortable. I asked him to make the steel ball into dense wood. He did that in about two seconds, and followed the fast pace of "chunking down" – OK from black to brown … OK make it into a medium-sized children's ball – OK, now a tennis ball. OK, now lighten the texture to polystyrene. OK, now change the colour to white. OK, now shrink the tennis ball to a golf ball. OK, now to a marble. OK, now to a tiny round mint. What can you do with that, Roy? "I can dissolve it Miss", he said.

It probably took him less than five minutes to transform the material that had been weighing him down for many years of his young life. I swear that he looked so much different the next time that we met. He seemed more mature, and somehow, more at peace.

Janet

Janet is the most difficult case that I have ever worked with using sub-modalities. She was in her mid twenties. Her mother rang me to say that she had a pain up her nostrils. She had gone to live in America and had married an American. She had received surgery for the pain up her nose not once, but three times. The pain was still there. Her mother said,

"She must have the clearest nostrils in the whole of the North American continent". When she arrived, I asked her to picture her discomfort. It was a huge, cubical weight far larger than her head. She 'chunked down' to make it smaller and smaller until it disappeared, although it did take us all session. She returned the next week scoring herself as being three out of ten better.

The next week, her discomfort still present, though to a lesser degree, she looked at it again. This time, she had a pain up her nose like two red-hot spears. She worked on this, 'chunking it down' and down until she made the spears were like spears of asparagus before she banished them completely. She returned feeling five out of ten better. Not bad after three unsuccessful surgical interventions. She then needed to work with feelings about her father who had divorced her mother three years or so before, which she was able to do on the way to making a full recovery.

Changing sub-modalities is a powerful technique that can be used no matter what the preferred representational system. First gain an impression of the situation - in other words, define the way you experience it. Then begin, one step at a time, to change the experience - always making it feel better. If you do something that makes you more uncomfortable, simply go back a step, and try something different.

Other NLP techniques

There are two more techniques that I have found very useful, and would like to share with you.

Swish

This technique involves closing your eyes and creating a picture in your mind of a situation you would like to change. The best example is something you do - a habit, or something like that, which you would rather not do. If you are not visual, it is good enough to get a sense of yourself doing whatever it is. Make this image or sense as complete as you can. Make it big, make it in full colour, make all the details as clear as you can. And in the bottom corner of this image put a little image of yourself doing what you would rather be doing. Let it be small and in black and white, and a little out of focus. If you have a sense of yourself, rather than a visual image, then imagine the other behaviour as a little seed at the bottom corner of the main sense. Hold that in your awareness for a moment, then count from 1 to 3, and say *'Swish'* and as you do so, draw the small image or seed up over the other one, covering it completely, and now experience the desired behaviour with clarity and vividness. When you have this perfectly, open your eyes and look around briefly. Then close your eyes and repeat the process - first the behaviour you would prefer to stop, then swish, the little image over the big one. Repeat this three or four times at a sitting, and repeat the whole activity a few times.

It may be easier to speak the process onto a tape, and follow your own instructions. Behaviours such as smoking, shouting or losing your temper, nail biting, and many others have been helped with this technique.

Circles of Excellence

Consider this a gift to yourself. Stand up, with your eyes open, and imagine a circle on the floor in front of you. Get a clear idea of what your circle looks like. Then step inside your circle, and close your eyes. Recall something that you did really well - some success or particular achievement - a time when you felt really good about yourself. Gather up all you can about this event. Recall, (or make up, if necessary) experiences from all your senses to go with it. When you have it clear in you mind, open your eyes, and step out of your circle.

Make sure your circle is still there, then step inside, and recall the same situation - how you felt, everything you can remember - making it even more vivid than before. Open your eyes and step out of the circle. Repeat this once or twice more. Then mentally fold up your circle and put it in your pocket. It works very much like the anchoring we described earlier. Imagine being able to recall that sense of success when you are nervous about speaking to a group, or stepping into the bank manager's office to ask for a loan! Just mentally unfold your circle and step into it.

Reframing

A very powerful way of moving towards a resourceful state is to *reframe* the experience in terms of the meaning it holds for us. This is best explained by the use of an example.

Mike

Mike was a war veteran. He wanted help to cope with a traumatic incident. He had been a marine in charge of a small group of men, and was the only survivor of a reconnaissance exercise into enemy lines. He found the fact of his survival difficult to deal with, and was accused, by his superior officers, of living while everyone else died. Many times he had to cope with the question, "How come you're the only one to return?" At times he wished he had died as well.

The therapist was able to help him change his perspective by stressing the importance of his survival in the light of what happened after the incident. Mike had been able to get back to base and provide information regarding enemy movements that had actually prevented a far larger group, the whole platoon of seventy men, from being caught in an ambush and probably killed. So instead of 'cheating death', Mike was able to see that his survival was in fact directly responsible for many other lives being saved. "I'd never thought of it like that" he said, and left the consulting room looking a whole lot lighter than when he came in.

By changing perspective on circumstances that cannot be changed, it is sometimes possible to find the circumstances a little easier to deal with. Basically the process is simple, and requires only a little lateral thinking. In Mike's case it was a question of taking his perception - that his life was a mistake - and using the exact opposite - in other words that his life was purposeful and important. Proof of this was easy to find - his survival resulted in many, many lives being saved.

A resourceful state can enhance communication skills in two ways. Firstly, by recognising the condition in ourselves, we can avoid projecting the way we feel outwards and confusing channels of communication between others and ourselves. "Re-resourcing" an internal state is an "internal" matter (unless in a relationship specifically designed for this purpose, for example a therapeutic relationship).

The second benefit lies in being able to recognise a resourced state in another person. If the other person is not in a resourced state, we are then able to make allowances for them, or assist them in the process of "re-resourcing" as appropriate.

10

Building External Relationships

Most of us have at one time or another felt really alone. We can be alone and isolated in the middle of the busiest supermarket or the funkiest party. In one sense we are alone - we come into the world alone, and we leave it alone. But on the way we can form bonds with people, we can meet them at really deep levels, and have a sense of being at-one with them. Both sex and religion have been used as temporary antidotes for isolation, but many people go through their lives largely unacknowledged and unseen.

Rudolph Steiner, philosopher and educationist, spoke of the need we all have to see ourselves in the world around us. He used this idea in the context of the development of individual will. In Steiner schools young children spend many years manipulating their environment, particularly in an artistic sense, so that they can see the imprint of their existence. Think of a young child doing finger painting - they are so proud of the hand or footprints that they produce - literally an imprint of their existence.

When the focus of our lives - as it is and must be - is on working to earn the crust for the table, we almost always find ourselves subservient to the task we perform. *We* don't matter - getting the job done does. As small cogs in large machines, our lives and our experiences are not acknowledged in any way. And no one listens to us. Whether or not we feel bad because of what happened to us as young children, things happen to us as adults, which can severely undermine even the highest level of self-confidence. This experience of not being listened to is potentially very damaging. It is difficult to get any sense of ourselves at all if our world seems to ignore us.

True listening is an art - and without listening, *really* listening, it is impossible to build a relationship - to meet someone where they are. True listening is a very powerful way of saying to another person, "You are important, your life and your experiences are important, and I want to share your reality with you". When we do this the other person feels valued and worth something. We would all like to be treated in this way, and the best way to make sure that this happens is to lead by example.

It is important to remember that real listening takes time, and time is precious to all of us. If you are busy and you can see that someone needs a listening space, it is better to schedule a little time later to do the job properly than to listen with only one ear. When we only half listen, the message that is received is the opposite of the one we need to give when we want to acknowledge someone. We say 'You're not important enough to listen to'. This does more harm than good, both to the other person and to our relationship with them.

Helping Methods

Not all problems are yours; so don't always take the responsibility. There have been people who have gone through the **Peace of Mind**™ training programme and taken only this piece of growth away with them, and have changed their lives drastically because of it, literally lifting a weight off their shoulders. One young woman in particular springs to mind. She said to me "If someone has a problem, I think I ought to fix it", and meant it with all her heart. She was a bright woman; as a teenager she had been a member of the National Youth Orchestra of Great Britain, no mean feat, then had trained as a solicitor. The gradual realisation, though, that she could relieve herself of having to solve all her colleague and friends' problems was like lifting a huge weight off her shoulders.

Do your best to find out who owns the problem. A child could have a problem like having no friends, being late for school every morning or wanting more pocket money. A parent may have a problem if a child does not work at school, or has their music on very loud, or has no hobbies to occupy them-self with, or always arrives home late at night. Identifying who owns the problem can help to decide what needs to be done about it.

Even if there's a problem between an older person and a younger one, such as a parent and child, to use one of the most difficult scenarios, then a problem solving method can be used. If your child has a problem, do your best to let the child speak. As a listener, listen carefully, giving room for the youngster (or other person) to express their emotions. It is really important not give your own interpretation or solution. It is always helpful to be accepting of someone's behaviour or words. Do your best to sit next to the child or other person and take time. Listen in silence. Non-verbal reactions like smiling, encouraging, or placing an arm around someone's shoulder can be helpful. Open questions like "What happened then?" or "Do you want to tell me more?" may help things flow. Listen to their feelings behind the words, prompting them if necessary with questions like: "Did that make you feel angry? Hurt? Power-less?"

You do not necessarily have to find a solution. Very often, by just listening carefully to even a young child, the child finds their own solutions; or there may not be a solution! There is always, though, comfort and warmth from being listened to, and having your problem shared. Remember, also, that your values have changed according to your experience and age. Do your best to have trust in younger people around you.

EXERCISE 21

HELPING AND THE SELF-FEEDBACK MODEL
(About 10 minutes would be appropriate for this exercise)

1. Listen to someone talking about what's important. (If you can do this with a partner, so much the better, so that you can learn and grow together).

2. Do your best to communicate acceptance and caring, concentrating on open questions, simple acknowledgements and acknowledging feelings.

3. After this either use either self or partner analysis in these terms:

   - What you did as the listener?
   - What you were pleased about?
   - What you felt?
   - What do you think was the effect on the other person in terms of their response?
   - What you could do differently next time?

Considering calmly your performance in this way can give us useful information and insights into how to perform better next time. If you're working with a partner, let them go through the questions above. Swap places, and do the exercise the other way round.

Questions

Questions are the easiest and often the quickest way to get to the bottom of something. They can be very effective when used correctly, but they can also do a great deal of harm. The key word here is speed - we get the information we want quickly. But what happens to the other person? Do they feel that what they have to say has value? Very often questions are for us, not for them. We use them because we want the information, and we want it in the order that we decide by our questions. Have you ever watched a small child struggling to carry a large object, and dashed over to help them, only to find that they were upset and cried in anger or frustration at your help? This is because they wanted to do it themselves. By taking away the challenge, we dis-empower the child. They were exploring their ability to manipulate their world. Often questions can have the same effect, and for the same reason.

Often too, the questions we use are *closed* questions, where there is a very limited range of possible answers, most often "yes" or "no".   If someone is struggling to get going, or to say what is on their mind, closed questions can be more of a hindrance than a help. If on the other hand we use *open* questions, we point the person in a direction, and allow them to get on with it. An open question encourages someone to explore an issue, or to think about something more deeply than they had before.

Even open questions should be used with discretion when we listen to someone else tell their story. They may pause for thought, and we may well barge in with a question, which they duly answer, but their original idea is gone, and they are distracted from their purpose. It is difficult to generalise, because questions are appropriate a lot of the time. What we have to ask ourselves is *why* we are asking the question? Here are a few of the less useful reasons we may do this:

- To fill silences that the **listener** finds uncomfortable.
- To confirm something the questioner is thinking.
- To veil some emotion or need of the questioner e.g. "Why are you doing that?" instead of "I don't want you to do that".
- To satisfy the questioner's own curiosity or need to know.

In each of these cases the focus was on the listener, and had very little to do with the speaker. If we relate that back to the concept of listening as being empowering and helping the other person to feel valued and cherished, we can see that questions can deliver the opposite message.

Getting into Listening Mode

For most of us real, attentive listening is very difficult. Even if we have the time and the desire to listen to someone, it is difficult to resist the urge to jump in with questions and advice. Advice can be very damaging to a relationship, especially when it goes wrong! If we remember that we each inhabit our own version of reality, it is obvious that our solution to a problem would be as unique to us as our perception of the problem. It the same with the person we are listening to. Learning to listen is a skill, just like learning to relax, or any of the other skills we have discussed in this book. It takes time and dedication to acquire it.

There are many things that might get in the way of real listening. The person we are listening to might beg us to help them - to tell them what to do. We may ourselves never have had the experience of being listened to, so we have nothing on which to model our behaviour, so we need to be kind to ourselves. Simply the awareness of what we are doing can be enough to steer us onto a different course, and bit by bit we can change the way we go about doing things. And the delightful thing about all this is that as we change, so those about us change, and the world ends up a better place.

Dr. M. Scott Peck, in his book *The Different Drum* (1988) illustrates this beautifully in a story called "The Rabbi's Gift". It is about an order of monks in a monastery in a forest. As these monks get older, they realise that their order is dying out because they have no new recruits. One day the abbot decides to visit a rabbi who sometimes goes on retreat in the forest, to discuss this problem. The rabbi is suitably understanding and the two old men shake their heads and commiserate with each other, but the rabbi is unable to shed any light on the abbot's problem. Before the abbot leaves, the rabbi says, as a parting shot, "The Messiah is one of you". Puzzled, the abbot returns to the monastery and he tells the monks what the rabbi said, including the last bit, about one of them being the Messiah. They shake their heads in puzzlement, and get on with their daily lives. But the germ of the idea the rabbi planted takes root in their mind, and they begin to wonder whether it's possible that one of them was the Messiah, and if so, to wonder whom the Messiah might be. The bottom line of the story is "As they contemplated in this manner the old monks began to treat each other with extraordinary respect on the off chance that one among them might be the Messiah. And on the off, off chance that each monk himself might be the Messiah, they began to treat themselves with extraordinary respect".

The result of this is that a great sense of respect and peace descends on the monastery, and people who visit the forest sense this, and come to like visiting the monastery. Before too long young men find themselves in conversation with the old monks, and after a little while one man, then another joins the order, saving it from extinction. In the same way, our behaviour and the way we treat others sets up the ripple effect we alluded to earlier, and before long, **Peace of Mind** belongs to us all!

What Makes a Relationship?

Some would say chemistry, or having something in common. But beyond this skill plays a part too. Just as in the monastery, if we treat each other with compassion and caring, we will find that we are able to get on together in a way that might surprise us.

Carl Rogers, who lived and worked earlier this century, dedicated his life to understanding the nature of relationship. He was primarily interested in the relationship between a therapist and their client, but the principles he set out are the same for all relationships. He identified three things, which he felt were fundamental to any relationship. He felt they were so important that he called them the *core conditions* for the existence of a relationship.

In the first place, he spoke about Unconditional Positive Regard. Translated into normal-speak, this can be called **acceptance.** By this he meant that in any relationship, both parties must feel that the other person accepts them for who they are. If we have strong negative feelings about the appearance, behaviour or any other aspect of the other person, they will get a sense of it and may well feel rejected and judged. They will certainly not feel that we understand them and so they will clam up, close up, and we will be unable to communicate with them in any real way. If we return to the previous chapter, and what we said about each one of us having our own, unique world - in order to let the other person feel accepted, we need to get into their world, their frame of reference, and we need to let them know that we are there for them.

Pause a moment and think of the implications of communicating acceptance to someone else. There are many questions we need to ask ourselves. Do we accept them? If not, why don't we? Do we have a problem with something universal, like race or sex, or do we have a problem with something they have done? If our problem is with their actions, why is this a problem? Do we think it makes them less of a person? Did we know we had this problem? In other words, we need to do a little self-exploration to discover the reasons behind our feelings, and then decide whether we find our reasons logical and in accordance with our belief system. Very often the feelings we have, and the reactions we have to other people are as a result of something buried in our unconscious minds. This can even be something we have accepted from other people, such as parents and friends and not thought about much. Perhaps now is a good time to examine any issues and decide whether they really belong to us.

Rogers also spoke of something he called **congruence.** The word means 'the same' and refers to the way we communicate. If we are congruent, what we feel and what we say are literally the same - in other words, we are honest about what we feel in a situation. If NLP is right, and 55% of our communication is non-verbal, and we are not quite honest about what we say, then we have to be very good actors to get away with it. It is arguable whether we ever get away with it, because as we've seen, most of this non-verbal communication goes on at a subconscious level, and even good actors can't influence what they don't know about.

Sometimes it is difficult to be congruent. What about when somebody is as pleased as punch with a new outfit, and you think they look awful? What can you do but pray they don't ask your opinion! Sometimes there can be a fine line between honesty and brutality. We are talking here about building relationships, not breaking them down, so congruence needs to be treated with the respect it deserves. When used correctly, it can be one of the most powerful tools in our relationship kit, but when used insensitively, it can lead to disaster.

1st person: "Excuse me, Mr Brown, do you have a moment? I have a bit of a problem".

2nd person: (frowning, apparently concentrating on a piece of paper in his hand) "Of course, any time. You know my door is always open. Sit down, sit down. Now what can I do for you?" (He continues to look down, even when 1st person speaks).

Mr Brown is being totally incongruent. His body language makes his feelings clear - that he is busy and hates being interrupted. Incongruence is easy to express and to illustrate. We may pretend to be interested in what someone says when we are in fact bored stiff. This is also incongruence. So we may nod, and smile and look at the person, but our thoughts may be on something else entirely.

The speaker invariably picks this up, even if it is on a subconscious level, and they instinctively begin to close off, protecting themselves from danger, because that is what incongruence does to a relationship. It breeds an air of distrust and of not being safe, and that is a recipe for disaster in a relationship.

Useful congruence on the other hand comes from responding to a gut feeling about what somebody else says. It can help to get to the feeling behind the words, and in this way help the other person get a clearer idea of the nature of their problem. I will illustrate the usefulness of congruence in the section that follows on "Reflective Listening".

The final core condition Rogers identifies is **empathy.** Now this is quite different from sympathy. Empathy is the sense the speaker gets that the listener is able to comprehend their world. So it is not necessary to have had the same experience as the speaker in order to feel and express empathy. As we discussed, there are many ways of entering the reality of another.

When a listener is being empathic, the speaker feels as if the listener is 'there for them'. Achieving all three core conditions is something counsellors and therapists train for a long time to do. Do not expect yourself to get there simply by reading these words. Be aware of yourself and what you do, and practise the practical techniques given below as often as you can, and you will be surprised at the progress you make.

Reflective Listening

Reflective listening is the skill of mirroring back to a person, in your own words and manner, what that person is saying to you. It works within the 7% words and 35% tonal zone of communication, just as pacing, mirroring and matching works on the non-verbal level. It allows the speaker to hear what they are saying, see what they are meaning and feel what is happening. Through this process they are empowered to come to a better understanding of themselves and their situation.

At its simplest level, reflective listening is a process of listening with full attention that includes repeating back to the speaker a shortened version of what they say. Most of us use this skill already when we are being given directions to get somewhere. We take in the information then say it back to the giver to check whether we have got it right. We are converting what we have said into our own words to make sure of our own understanding. With reflective listening we are doing the same thing but with the emphasis on helping the other person to get a clearer idea about what is going on for them. It also goes a long way towards preventing misunderstandings - we often think or feel we understand what a person has said but this is just guesswork, unless we check our understanding out with the speaker. When your words mirror clearly what is being said, you will get a clear "yes" response. If you miss the mark, the speaker will correct you. If you used a question to elicit the information, there is no guarantee that what you heard is what the speaker said.

There are subtly different ways to reflect what a person says. One method is to repeat the last word, the last few words, or the key words that a speaker says. For instance:

> Speaker: "And then she told me she was going to leave me".
> Listener: "Leave you".

Notice the difference in meaning if you turn it into a question. "Leave you?" can express astonishment, or it can express disbelief. If we don't believe what the other person says, we are judging them, we are effectively calling them liars, and that totally destroys our acceptance of them, which has the effect of breaking down the rapport between speaker and listener. Another example is:

> Speaker: "I was really upset when I heard about the accident".
> Listener: "You were upset".

At first it may feel a little strange to do this, but practice doing it and you will find, as I have, that it has two important effects on the speaker.

Firstly, it makes them feel that you are listening to them, and this makes them relax and feel safe, and secondly, it encourages them to carry on, or to expand on what they were saying. Very often their response to your reflection will be "Yes and ......", or they will nod, and continue their train of thought, (Think here what we said about asking questions. If we use a question at this point, it takes them in the direction *we* want them to go in). In terms of the core conditions, when we reflect in this way, we express both acceptance and empathy. It is in fact a very safe way of letting the speaker know that you are there.

We can also paraphrase what the other person says. This falls into the category mentioned earlier, about getting directions. When we paraphrase the meaning of the message, we make sure we understand what the person says, and we give them the message that we are really listening to them. Paraphrasing carries a little more risk in terms of communicating acceptance than does the simple reflection of words. We may get it wrong, and although the speaker will correct us, if we do this often, such as if we are not really listening properly, they will begin to feel unimportant, and that we do not accept them. They will also begin to realise that there is a gap between what we say and what we feel. Our incongruence may start to show!

People who speak to us and need us to use our listening skills usually want to speak about how they feel about something. There will be a story there, but the reason they need to speak is that there is a feeling underneath the story. Some people chatter on, masking their feelings by many words. Other people are able to express the way they feel easily. If our speaker falls into this category, it is relatively easy to listen to them, and to get a good idea of what is going on for them. If they are of the former variety, listening can be quite tough. Remember that in listening to them, we not only want to make them feel at ease, but in order to be really useful to them, we need to present them with a mirror image of themselves. So if they are not saying what they are feeling, it can be very useful for us to help them to recognise their feelings. This involves listening carefully to their words, observing what their bodies are saying to us, and then reflecting, very diplomatically, what we think they are feeling. Sometimes their words may even say the opposite of what they are feeling. For example:

> Speaker: "I really don't care what she says. She's always criticising me, and telling me I'm not good enough for her son. And I've tried to be nice, but I just don't care anymore."

> Listener: "It seems to me that you are really hurt by the way she treats you."

The speaker has said nothing about being hurt - she probably sounds rather angry, and it would be easy to collude with her, and to say that you think her mother-in-law is really awful. By identifying the feeling behind the words, you will probably cause her to look inside herself, past her indignation and frustration, and discover that she is hurting rather badly. Of course, you may be quite wrong, and she may only be angry. If this is the case, she will correct you, just as if you had made a mistake paraphrasing her words.

The listener's response was probably based on a gut feeling gleaned from both conscious and unconscious body language, tone, and what was said before, and as such it represents a congruent response. When what we pick up is different to what the other person feels, and we are congruent about it - in other words we say what we feel - it can make them feel that we are judging them. As with the simple reflecting of worlds, we need to be careful that our words do not reflect incredulity or surprise or accusation when we say something "controversial".

In the above example, had the speaker responded in terms of the anger and frustration, she would not necessarily have been incongruent. She may have responded in this way if she did not notice the underlying hurt, or she may have noticed it, but was biding her time, waiting for more evidence to support her hunch, or for a better moment to make her comment. This is the nature of congruence.

In most cases it is better to wait until there is relative certainty before saying something which may be challenging. Sometimes we are not aware of what we actually feel, or why we feel it, and so we may need a little time to sort out what is happening inside of us before we attempt to lay it onto the other person. In the above example, if the listener had a similar experience of being treated badly by her own mother-in-law, or anyone else for that matter, those feelings of hurt and anger and frustration may have been activated inside herself, and she may have responded more on her own account than on account of the speaker. If the speaker was only angry, and the listener was hurt, the reflection of feeling would have been wrong and inappropriate. The listener may have been better advised to wait until the speaker presented more evidence as to how she really felt.

So we can see, reflecting feelings, especially hidden feelings, although potentially useful and powerful, can pose quite a significant danger to acceptance and empathy, and should be done with care and awareness.

Another way of reflecting is to use an NLP reframe. Using it in the context of communication with another person is similar to using it ourselves to achieve a resourced state, but it does require some very careful handling. Of all the methods of reflective listening, this is by far the most dangerous in relation to Roger's core conditions. We are probably all familiar with people who always try to cheer us up, urging us to look at the half full bottle, rather than the half empty one, or to tell us that it may never happen. These are reframes, turning our view around to a more positive one. But remember how these people make us feel. Angry? Frustrated? That they don't understand what it's like for us? This is what reframes do when they are used incorrectly. They usually come from someone who is tired of listening to us, and wants to shut us up.

If we have ever had an experience like this, we will probably acknowledge that they had a point, and that we may have been carrying on a bit about something. But we don't feel very good about ourselves at the time, and we certainly don't feel confident about our relationship with the person who has introduced the reframe.

Sometimes people get so deep into despair, or find a set of circumstances so difficult to cope with that they end up going around in circles. Or sometimes their behaviour is locked into an illogical sequence as a result of faulty thinking on their part. At these times, skilful use of a reframe may help them to find a way out of their impasse. Skilful use has two distinct steps. First it is important to acknowledge just how difficult / awful / uncomfortable the situation is. In other words, it is essential to communicate very clearly that you are able to understand the world of the other person as they experience it. You need to communicate both acceptance and empathy unambiguously. The second step - and this can be in the same sentence as the first, is to suggest that there is another way of looking at things - the reframe. Without the first step, this strategy is almost always disastrous, but with it, it becomes a powerful way of helping someone over a wall.

It must be stressed that these are practical skills, and as such don't work all that well on paper. It is essential to try and try and try again, and over time you will grow into a good listener.

Roadblocks in communication

So many of our communication skills are 'picked up' from the modelling we had from parents – the unconscious messages from them that, "This is the way to do it". We must be easy with ourselves therefore, gentle and accepting that we are making changes the best way we can. How many of these next points are familiar to you? How did you feel when things like this were said?

Giving orders "You must go to the shop immediately", or, "Go and take the dog for a walk straight away".

Accusing "You never tidy up your room", or, in the case of a second marriage where both have birth children, "Why is it that it's always MY children who've done something wrong?"

Preaching "Young people must have respect for older people".

"Old time" talking "I remember when I was young I always had to be in at half-past nine, even on a Saturday night".

Giving Solutions Use of the phrase "you should" as a way of offering a bit of advice. Whilst this is intended to be helpful, giving the solution is about the giver of the solution and not about the person being related to, as previously mentioned. One persons' "helpfulness" can so often be disempowerment to the person receiving the message.

Comforting Phrases such as "you must not take this so seriously" might not actually be comforting, even though they are intended to be so. Such phrases often lead to resentment, accompanied by thoughts to the effect of "what actually do you know about it anyway?"

Rationalising Statements which use words such as "the facts are actually x, y, or z" can often leave people feeling insulted.

Threatening "If you leave me, I shall kill myself" is not an unfamiliar retort amongst some parting couples.

Praising "You can do this so well, so why don't you do this extra thing also!" (See also Appendix 7, page 167 for "Realising the 'Small Peace' between Parents and Children - 10 Points of View").

Challenging

Being a good listener does not mean that we allow everyone to dump their problems onto us. Sometimes we find ourselves faced with behaviours - verbal or non-verbal - that infringe on our rights as human beings. These are times when we need to be totally congruent about the way we feel, and find useful ways of expressing ourselves. The best outcome of such a situation is to get the person to stop what they are doing that causes us distress. Of course we can choose to lose our temper, and then they will probably do the same, and we will both walk away feeling awful about ourselves, and the problem will not be resolved.

One of the things that we need to consider in relation to the subject of challenging is our desired outcome. I suspect that what most of us want is to get our own way, and to have a fairly quiet life rather than a great row doing it. Remember a time when someone told you off. Did you want to change your behaviour or did you feel resentful?

EXERCISE 22

HOW YOU WERE CHALLENGED IN THE PAST
(This will take you about 15 minutes)

1. Think back to a time in the past, if possible from childhood or teens.
2. Remember times when you were told off by an adult for doing something that they didn't like you doing.
3. How did they challenge you?
4. What did they say?
5. What do you remember about their non - verbal communication?
6. How did you react and feel?
7. Did you want to change what you were doing as a result?

First a word about "I" messages. They are a way of us owning up to how we feel about a situation and keeping feelings 'clean', for example "I feel angry" rather than "You make me feel angry". With "I" messages, I have a problem, so that's what I must say! "I'm very worried when you come home so late; I cannot sleep because I keep thinking that something may have happened to you. I would like you to tidy up your room, because I want to clean it today and I can't do it when everything is on the floor. I feel very angry that you did not keep your promise". An "I" message may be giving your own opinion and it could be responsive, preventive, positive or confronting.

It may be helpful to isolate situations where this has happened to you – so look at exercise 23 below.

This next method is a problem-solving one for specific needs and is useful for two or more people who need to negotiate together. Firstly, take time to both name your problem with a clear "I" message. Make sure that you know exactly what your need is. Together, brainstorm all possible (and even impossible!) solutions. You may write them down; make no judgements yet. Look at each solution you have written down and say whether you think it will work or not. Choose a solution you both think will work. Write down your agreed arrangements. Work with the solution you decided on. After some time, have an evaluation. What works, what does not work? If you are both satisfied, continue. If not, then start the procedure again until you are both satisfied. I have found a little strategy called the 4-part "I" challenge to be most effective in these situations. It works as follows:-

---

EXERCISE 23

TO EXPLORE SITUATIONS WHERE YOU WERE NOT GETTING YOUR NEEDS MET
(This should take about 15 minutes)

1. Think of situations where you have a problem with a person's behaviour.
2. Ask yourself the following questions and note down the answers: -

- Whose problem is it?
- What is the other person doing?
- What effect is it having on me? (Or what is the consequence of the behaviour?)
- How do you feel about the effect?

3. Then do another situation - do it on your own in your head and then write it down, so that the process becomes more and more automatic.
4. Do as many situations as possible.

Let us assume a hypothetical problem:

Alan drinks a lot of coffee from the office vending machine, and leaves the disposable cups in a trail behind him. Everyone in the office is fed up with his selfish behaviour and the coffee rings he has left on countless documents. In spite of many pleas to reform, he continues this practise. This morning you returned to your desk to find a coffee ring on an important document you were working on.

Once we have determined where the problem lies (see Chapter 4), we can issue our challenge:

1. State the offending behaviour without using labels:

"Alan, when you leave your empty and sometimes not so empty coffee cups wherever you go..."

2. State the effect the behaviour has in the largest, most global sense you can:
    "...Someone else has to clean up after you, and you leave ugly coffee stains all over the place. This morning for instance you ruined the report I was working on for Mr Jones, and I've had to start all over again!"

3. State what you feel about the effect of the behaviour:
    "It is annoying to have to throw your cups away, and at the moment I feel really angry, because now I have to start the report all over, which means I've lost an hour of work."

4. Enlist their co-operation to change the situation:
    "I'm sure you don't do it deliberately, so is there some way we can work around your forgetfulness or whatever causes the problem, to make sure that this doesn't happen again?"

Ideally, Alan will be sorry, and a series of strategies can be devised that will help everyone to feel better.

Of course the 4 part "I" is not a "solve-all" solution, but it works in many instances where the initial reaction is one of anger and can often result in a "thank you for telling me that" kind of response.

Benedict

My son Benedict was, unfortunately, asthmatic as a youngster. I used to pick him up from school. One day, aged about 12, he was there with a few friends who all piled into my car for a lift back to the next village. They were twittery and on top notes. One of the teachers in a practical lesson had shouted at them very much, hitting one boy and making him cry. He had poked Ben in the chest several times whilst making a point. The boys seemed very bothered.

I thought for a good few days what to do, which way to leap. I had got on reasonably well with the teacher, who was at the end of a chain sending things to a Romanian orphanage, and I used to trot into school now and again with collected recyclable goodies to give him. Our rapport therefore seemed to have a reasonable start! I decided to go and see him, having assembled and rehearsed the best 4 part "I" that I could.

EXERCISE 24

FOUR PART CHALLENGING "I" MESSAGE
(This should take about 20 minutes)

1. Come up with a 4-part "I" message along the lines of the material given to you above.

2. Make sure that the message contains all 4 parts.

3   Practise saying the message to a mirror (or role-play to a partner or friend) then give yourself feedback on things like, the language used, tone of voice, body language and congruence.

4. In turn, imagine saying the message to a particular person or in a particular situation in the future – give yourself constructive feedback.

A friend or partner can also ask: "What do you need to do to ensure it is most likely to succeed?"

"When I collected the boys on (whatever day), you had shouted at them uncharacteristically and frightened and confused them. Ben tells me too that you poked him rather severely in the chest, and I'm rather bothered about that, since he is asthmatic. I just wonder what, between us, we can do about this situation?" (All the parts are there, can you find them?)

The reply came from the teacher who had acted uncharacteristically. I felt sorry for him as he told me the part of the story that I was unaware of - that the boys had had Miss X for the lesson before break and had been horrid to her. She had sobbed all over him in the staff room at break time. He had gone into see them for his lesson and was already angry with them, going in to them 'all guns blazing' unbeknownst to them. He said that he hadn't meant to frighten them, and would say that he was sorry next time he saw them. He then thanked me for being straight with him!

One of our trainees, a wonderful Dutch woman called Maria Brown, a very experienced therapist, and exceptional human being, extended the 4-part "I" message into a 6-part "I". She would always acknowledge before and after with, "I wonder if you would give me a minute?" and then after a 'yes' answer "Thank you". At the end, again she would acknowledge "Thank you for listening to me about this".

EXERCISE 25

TO CONTINUE TO DEVELOP AN UNDERSTANDING OF PROBLEM OWNERSHIP AND TO RAISE AWARENESS OF HOW BEHAVIOUR THAT WE DON'T LIKE AFFECTS US
This should take about 15 minutes thinking time

1. Think of a couple of examples of other people's behaviour that you have tried to challenge without noticeable effect or things you think would be a waste of time trying to challenge.

2. As you come up with an example, ask yourself:

    - Who owns the problem in this situation - you, the other person or both?
    - What is the concrete and tangible effect on you of the other person's behaviour?

There are occasions where no amount of reasonableness oils the wheels of discord. Some people are just not open to listening, no matter how reasonable we are. In these cases it is often better to walk away with our sense of self intact, rather than to engage with someone who bears us ill. If it is possible, we should avoid contact with people who are totally unwilling to communicate with us in a reasonable manner. If we are unable to avoid them, the only way to retain some semblance of dignity is to chip away at them with strategies such as the one above, and to trust that in time they will hear, and move to a more reasonable position.

Another very useful strategy to use is what I call the "Soft No". This is for those times when somebody tries to push us in a direction that we do not wish to go. It can be an overbearing boss, a workmate, a friend, or a family member who does not want to listen to and accept our position. Often in these situations tempers and voices can becomes a little heated, and rise, or get louder.

The first thing to do is to cause your voice to do exactly the opposite. Instead of raising your voice, lower it. Each time you speak, speak more softly, and with quiet emphasis. Do not let your tone get excited, or join the other person in their anger or excitement.

EXERCISE 26

**TO GIVE YOURSELF AN EXPERIENCE OF BEING
<u>FIRM</u> WHILST STAYING <u>CALM</u>**
(This should take you 10 minutes)

1. Think of a situation where you would want to say NO but usually end up giving in.

2. If you can (but it isn't essential) get someone to help you by role playing the other person.

3. Keeping calm inside, keep your needs clearly in mind, and believe that the other person will accept what you say. Be completely straight. Do not offer explanations, and if they get loud and angry, try getting softer and quieter and even whispering.

4. If someone is role playing the other person, try to influence the outcome.

5. Try to make things as real as possible. Helper, coach if necessary!

6. Give yourself feedback, and helper, if there, give feedback as well.

You may like to repeat this exercise until it feels completely fluent.

And each time they entreat you, or urge you, just say "No", more and more quietly and congruently. If it is a social occasion, and you are being urged for example to go somewhere, or to have another drink, and you say "no", and laugh with everyone else, you are not being congruent, and they will realise this, and press you harder. But saying "no" in a quiet, firm tone will convey the seriousness of your intentions, emphasising that you mean what you say. This technique is particularly good with children who persist in begging for something when it has been refused.

Both the 4-part "I" and the "soft no" are deceptively simple. They don't need years of practise to perfect, and their effectiveness has been proved over and over again. Try it for yourself.

11

A Final Word

Having come this far in our quest for **Peace of Mind,** you probably realise that it is not something that someone else can give to you, nor can it be bought at any price. It is something that we create by our awareness, our honesty and our desire to make the world a better place. To have **Peace of Mind** we need to feel good inside and to help others feel good as well. By treating others as we wish to be treated we give them permission to act in a different way themselves. In this way **Peace of Mind** echoes and spreads around us just like a tiny "trimtab" changes the course of a mighty tanker. Harold Willens explains (from his book *The Trimtab Factor: How Executives can help solve the Nuclear Weapons Crisis* - William Morrow Company, New York, 1984):

"On airplane wings, and on the keels of racing yachts, trimtabs are small adjustable flaps that assist in balancing and steadying the motion of the craft. The principle of the trimtabs also applies to a ship's rudder. In explaining the trimtab factor (the late) Buckminster Fuller (architect, inventor, and philosopher) used the image of a large ocean going ship travelling at high speed through the water. The mass and momentum of such a vessel are enormous, and great force is required to turn the rudder and change the ship's direction. In the past some large ships had, at the trailing edge of the main rudder, another tiny rudder, the trimtab. By exerting a small amount of pressure, one person could easily turn the ship. Thus the trimtab factor demonstrates how the precise application of a small amount of leverage can produce a powerful effect."

Those of us that are old enough will remember the London smog, which happened on many occasions in the 1950s and early 1960s. Smog was a natural fog with things trapped in it – fumes from industrial sites, car exhausts, domestic coal, coke and so on. There were many more deaths than there should have been for an equivalent time without fog. The government of the time brought in legislation fairly quickly in the shape of the clean air act. Some of the populace of London was outraged. How could their lighting a coal fire POSSIBLY make any difference? But it did. As the legislation was adhered to, the air became clean, and a difference was made. Individual actions brought about collective change.

One person *can,* you see, make a difference. We must believe it in the deepest part of ourselves. If we do believe this, and as a consequence do not make any effort, then it is a sad world that awaits our children and our children's children. In our small corner of the world we can make a difference, and like the trimtab, this can change the entire direction of the world.

Do remember the inspiration from that amazing man, Nelson Mandela, whose life is a testimony to his belief, expressed in the following extract from his inaugural address as President of South Africa:

"Our deepest fear is not that we are inadequate.
Our deepest fear is that we are powerful beyond measure.
It is our light, not our darkness that most frightens us.
We ask ourselves, who am I to be brilliant, gorgeous, talented, fabulous?
Actually, who are you not to be?
You are a child of God.
Your playing small doesn't serve the world.
There is nothing enlightened about shrinking so that other people won't feel insecure around you.
We are all meant to shine, as children do.
We were born to make manifest the glory of God that is with us.
It is not in some of us, it's in everyone.
And as we let our own light shine, we unconsciously give others permission to do the same.
As we are liberated from our fear, our presence automatically liberates others."

I wish you and your world **Peace of Mind.**

APPENDICES

APPENDIX 1

THE SOUND OF CALM – a meditational approach to suggestibility

By Sue Washington (with thanks to the late Dr. John Hartland, Emeritus President of the British Society for Medical and Dental Hypnosis and Dr. Don W. Ebrahim)

Approximately 30 minutes

I want you to sit in the chair and look straight in front of you. Let your eyes wander upwards towards a spot on the ceiling, a real spot or an imaginary spot, and stay fixed on that spot. Count backwards in your head, not out loud from 300. When you reach 295, let your eyes close, and you can stop counting... Let your eyelids feel heavy and limp.... Then, I want you to say the word CALM in your head, gently, with each breath that you breathe out.... CALM.... CALM.... Don't bother to give it any meaning, repeat it as a sound, like the sound of a distant bell in your head...and as you repeat the sound of calm, gently in your mind with each breath that you breathe out, so all your mind and body is becoming calm.

A time will come when you may find that sound of CALM fading out of your mind because you're listening to me, and as soon as you notice that, bring the sound of CALM back, gently, and keep repeating it.... But then, a time will come, when you're so calm and relaxed, that you don't have the mental energy to bring it back again, and when that time comes, then let the sound of calm go, and let yourself go.... into the deepest and most pleasant relaxed state you've ever, ever been in, in your life....

So now, let the heaviness and relaxation from your eyelids flow up through your eyebrows, over your forehead...over the top of your head and down the back of your head and neck... Let that happen NOW... and each time you hear me use the word NOW, like that, you let every bit of relaxation that you produce, become more and more complete...

So NOW... let that heaviness and relaxation flow down your face...down your cheeks and nose, round your mouth and chin, and down the front of your neck. Let your head go ... surrender it to the gentle support that is behind it (or let it rest upon your shoulders)...

Let your back muscles go... let them slump down limp and slack and heavy... and let that heaviness and relaxation flow down into your chest... let your chest muscles relax, and feel your breathing getting easier and more gentle and more natural now. And as you repeat the sound of CALM, gently with each breath that you breathe out, so your chest muscles are relaxing, and your breathing is getting easier and easier now...

NOW... let your shoulders go...let them slump down, limp and slack, and heavy...and let that heaviness and relaxation flow down through your arms...

through your upper arms and elbows, lower arms and wrists, hands and fingers...down to the tips of your fingers...to the tiniest muscles there...

And then, let the relaxation move downwards through your trunk... And let that relaxation flow down round your waist, down through your tummy...down through your bottom and all the way round your hips.... Down through your upper legs and thighs, knees, lower legs, ankles and feet, down to the very tiniest muscles at the end of your toes...

And in a moment I am going to count from 10 to 1... And as I count, so you let yourself go.... Let yourself go... let your self drift down through 10 levels of relaxation and rest without any effort, just as though you are gliding down on a moving staircase.... until you get to the point at which you're more relaxed than you've been for a long, long time, maybe more relaxed than you've ever been, but remembering that you're the one that is in control, as relaxed as you want to be and are able to let yourself be at this session today..... So ready...10, 9, 8, 7, 6, 5, 4, 3, 2, 1.....

So, each time that you hear me use the word NOW like that.... you go twice as deeply into relaxation and rest.

And NOW.... as you let go and rest more and more deeply, that calm is spreading out into every cell, into every tissue, and into every muscle of your body..... and as calm is spreading out into every cell, every tissue, every muscle of your body, so your muscles are relaxing and continuing to relax..... and as your muscles are relaxing so they may feel heavy.... and as your muscles feel heavy.... so your body feels heavy too... soon I hope your body feels so lovely and limp and relaxed and heavy, that its almost as though parts of your body have faded away.... as if they don't belong to you any more..... and because that has such a very pleasant feeling, you are able to let go and go deeper still into relaxation and rest ....

And NOW, as you let go.... rest deeper and deeper.... so this is helping you.... every day.... in lots of ways to feel better .... to feel stronger and to feel fitter.... because in this deep rest you are storing up calm, and calm is energy.... and so you will find.... you do become.... much more awake ... much more vibrant ..... much more energetic.... having much more zest for life

And NOW.... as you let go and rest deeper and deeper so this is helping you..... every day.... to feel your mind getting.... calmer and clearer.... more composed..... more placid .... more tranquil.... You will be able to see things more clearly.... to concentrate more easily.... and as a result.... your memory will improve ... and you will be able to see things in their true perspective.... clearly and concisely.... able to look at the bright side of things when the choice arises..... which it does so very, very often.... and because of this, every day.... you'll feel a greater feeling of personal happiness and well being .... a greater feeling of personal safety and security than you have felt for a long, long time ....

And NOW.... as you rest deeper.... and deeper ... so this is helping you every day.... to feel.... much more calm ... and so very much more relaxed ... And as you become ....and as you remain.... much more calm.... and so very much more relaxed ... so you will develop... much more confidence.... in yourself.... much more confidence .... in your ability .... to do not only what you have to do each day .... but also much more confidence in your ability to do all those things that you know you ought to be able to do... knowing that you can do those things.... knowing that you have control of yourself.... knowing that you can change the world.... all that is important is NOW and breath you take.

And because of this.... every day.... you will feel more and more independent.... more able to stick up for yourself.... to stand upon your own two feet.... and to hold your own ... in any circumstances ....

And because these things will happen ... exactly as I tell you they will happen.... you are going to feel much happier.... much more cheerful and optimistic.... much more in control..... and much brighter generally ....To be CALM inside gives you more **Peace of Mind.**

Every day I want you to practice this relaxation technique for 20 minutes in the morning.... and 20 minutes in the late afternoon or evening.... the morning session prepares you for the activities of the day.... and the afternoon or evening session prepares you for the activities of the evening.... and the deep sleep of night time ....

All you'll do is to sit in the chair and look straight in front of you... you'll let your eyes roll upwards without moving your head towards a spot on the ceiling.... a real spot or an imaginary spot ....

As you gaze at the spot on the ceiling.... you will not let your eyes wander away from it for a single moment.... and as you gaze at the spot on the ceiling.... you'll count backwards to your self, not out loud, from 300.... and as soon as you reach 295.... you'll let your eyes close, and you'll stop counting ....

As soon as your eyes have closed and you have stopped counting.... you'll repeat the sound of calm ever so gently in your mind with each breath that you breathe out.... you will not bother to give it any meaning ... you'll repeat it like the sound of a distant bell in your head ....

As you repeat the sound of calm ever so gently with each breath that you breathe out.... so your mind and your body will very quickly begin to feel calm, just as calm as it is NOW, so calm that parts of your body will begin to feel as though they don't belong to you.... just though they have faded away.... and this usually begins in the hands and spreads to other parts of the body.... and because this is such a pleasant feeling.... you'll forget all about your body.... and go deeper.... and deeper.... into rest....

As you repeat this sound of calm ever so gently with each breath that you breathe out ... so you'll find many thoughts coming into your head.... let the thoughts come.... don't try to stop them.... but as soon as you notice that the sound of calm has faded out of your mind.... then gently bring it back again.... and keep repeating it.... and as you do so.... you go deeper into rest....

As soon as 20 minutes have passed you'll have an automatic urge to open your eyes.... but before opening your eyes.... you'll give yourself some positive suggestions.... for a few seconds to a minute before opening your eyes....

You may want to give your self a general suggestion.... by repeating the words "calm".... "confidence".... "calm".... "confidence".... "courage"....

(at the second session) You might want to be more specific... I WILL do this....

Whatever suggestion or suggestions you decide to give yourself.... they'll work just as strongly.... just as powerfully.... just as truly and surely.... as though I were giving them to you myself ....

During your relaxation session... you'll hear many noises and sounds of everyday life and living.... but they will not disturb you

But if anything should happen.... to threaten your privacy or your safety.... your eyes will open immediately and you will take precautions to safeguard yourself....

So NOW.... let yourself sink into the feeling of calm.... let yourself feel this feeling of calm washing over you.... let yourself become aware of the vastness of calm .... There are no boundaries.... no frontiers.... calm goes on... and on.... and on....

Let your self drift deeper.... and deeper.... into those deeper depths ....And listen to the inner peace and silence in that inner calm...the silence ... that whispers.... "calm".... "calm"...."calm"....

Rest very deeply now.... rest very comfortably now.... (Silence for 30/40 seconds)

In a moment I will count from one to seven.... and when I reach the count of seven.... you will come out of this deep rest.... and you 'you'll retain as much of the calm and relaxation as you need.

All the heaviness will leave your muscles.... they will feel much better for the rest....
And the next time that you listen to these words (or to your tape) you'll enter into this state.... very much more quickly and easily..... and you'll reach a level of rest very much deeper than this one ....So ready,

1...2...3...4...5...6...7... Open your eyes.

APPENDIX 2

VISUALISATION – THE VALLEY
By William Carr

Approximately 45 minutes

Now I want you to just allow yourself to relax... first of all, allowing those eyelids of yours to just gently relax...so that eventually you find that you just can't open them...you test them, and you just can't open them.

Now taking 5 good breaths.... Now you are allowing your unconscious mind to just drift away into daydreams; into pleasant, happy thoughts, maybe of the past.... Memories, memories of good times.... or of the future, just looking forward to things you hope for, things that you expect.....or indeed just think of the present - sunshine dappling through the trees, the memories of snow on the hills... the beauties of Spring, of Summer, of Autumn, of Winter....or even, perhaps, music in your head, the kind of music you like.....

Now you are allowing your conscious mind to drift away...into those daydreams. From now on, you are not listening to what I say, you are not listening to any of the sounds around you, you are not concerned with anything but your own self.... and it's almost as though you are wrapping yourself in your own cocoon....turning your back on the world for a little while...

And so you are allowing your body to relax, from the top of your head to the tips of your toes.... From the top of your head to the tips of your fingers...from the crown of your head, down to the back of your neck, down those comparatively big muscles at the back of your neck, ...with which you spend your time just holding your head up proudly and high, ...so that your head can, if it wishes, move to the right.... to the left...But if it becomes uncomfortable for your head to be in one position, you can tighten up those muscles for a little while, and move your head to a more comfortable position, and relax those muscles ....and the same goes for any part of your body....if it becomes uncomfortable, then you can move into a more comfortable position.....

Down now, from your neck muscles to those muscles across your shoulders.... down those two sets of muscles down your neck and across your shoulder-blades, the ones which most show the signs of stress and tension .. you are allowing them, gently, gently, steadily, steadily slowly, slowly to relax....

And now from the shoulder-blades down to the muscles on either side of your spine, all the way down to the small of your back, over your hips and the backs of your thighs, through the bend of your knees, and into your calves, through the back of your ankles and into those of your heels, those at the bottom of your feet, right to the tip of every toe....

Now from the top of your head once more, over the muscles of your forehead, your temples, over the muscles of your face around your eyes; those muscles which we sometimes wrinkle up in concentration and concern, or indeed, when we are trying to look at something which is too small for us to really make out....

Now these muscles are relaxing in a special way, flattening out against the structure of your face....

Now over the muscles of your eyes themselves; underneath those closed lids, there in the twilight, no need for them to focus; indeed no reason for them to move at all, so they are resting, relaxing. And down from your eyes, now, over the muscles of your cheeks to those of the mouth - your smiling muscles - and outwards from there to your jaws, somewhere at the bottom of your ears. As those jaw muscles relax, so your lower jaw parts company with the other; in other words, your teeth aren't touching. As the jaw muscles relax, so they help the other muscles of your face to relax.

Over your chin now, into the muscles of your throat, the muscles inside your throat - the ones we use to swallow, the ones we use to clear our throats - and the muscles on the outside of your throat. So now the whole of your head and the whole of your neck, which includes your face and your throat, and includes that wonderful part of you, your brain - all that is feeling warm and comfortable, and heavy, heavy.... and drowsy, drowsy, drowsy....

Down from your throat to the muscles of your chest, always working without pause, every minute of each day, working, working, working as your lungs expand and relax; those lungs which are always working, working every minute of every day. All those parts of your body which have been working since birth, and will do throughout life, maintaining good health, maintaining life itself.

Those continually working parts of your body, as Indeed any other parts of your body when they move, are using tension, muscular tension, and that, of course, is necessary tension, that goes on all the time. That other stuff we dignify with the name of tension, anxiety, that's unnecessary   As you allow yourself to relax, so that unnecessary tension is just drifting away, seeping away, away into the past where it really belongs.

And as your lungs relax, so like every other part of your body in relaxation, they become more and more efficient; so now, in relaxation, without any extra effort on your part, your lungs are taking in just that little bit more air, and within that air, of course, life-giving oxygen. So, just through that, you are feeling , and being, just that little bit fitter, healthier, stronger...so your heart, that wonderful muscular pump, pumping, pumping away, like your lungs but at a different rhythm, pumping newly oxygenated blood throughout your body by way of relaxed arteries....and that same blood coming back for re-oxygenation through relaxed veins....

And as your relaxed heart is pumping away, pumping your blood throughout your body, so your blood pressure is normalised.

And now, your stomach and digestive organs.... We have all experienced, at some time or other, that feeling that we can't eat; we're so tense, so upset, so

angry that we can't eat a thing; but now, in relaxation, your stomach and digestive organs are digesting all the food, taking all the goodness from that food, so that only the waste products are excreted; and so again, you are feeling and being fitter, healthier, stronger....

Now your liver and your kidneys, getting rid of the poisons more efficiently in your relaxed state, and again you are fitter, healthier, stronger. So down then from your rib cage to that wonderful muscular arrangement, your diaphragm, something that we always think we know how to relax when things get bad, with a good shout, or a good scream; with a cry, perhaps, or on certain occasions with a good belly laugh.

Down from your diaphragm to your abdominal muscles, your pelvic muscles, to the muscles at the front of your thighs, and over the knee joints to the muscles of your lower legs, the front of your ankles, to the tops of your feet: and again, to the tip of every toe.

Now across the top of your shoulders into the muscles of your upper arms, through the crook of your elbows into your forearms, through your wrists and into your hands, right to the tip of every finger, right to the tip of each thumb. Now steadily, steadily, slowly, slowly, relax...Relax in the whole of your body, from the top of your head to the tips of your fingers, from the top of your head to the tips of your toes.

Every single muscle, every single sinew, every single tendon, every single organ large and small, every single artery, every single vein, every single joint, every single nerve is relaxing.... Gently, steadily, relaxing.

It's almost as though you are lying down on an old-fashioned feather bed, sinking down, down deeper, deeper, deeper, feeling warm and comfortable ...heavy.

Heavy and drowsy, relaxing, drowsy. Asleep, yet not asleep; not asleep, yet not awake; sinking down, down, down until, feather beds being what they are, you find yourself floating, floating on feathers, floating on feathers which are lighter than you are, yet which hold you, gently hold you, floating, floating; floating as you did before you were born, floating in the comfortable purple darkness, lulled by the sound of your mother's heartbeat; floating, floating, now, as then, warm, comfortable and absolutely safe.... floating, floating now, deeper now, floating and sinking - sounds like a contradiction in terms, but it's not.

You are floating now, just like a bird, floating with outstretched, wonderful wings, floating and sinking, round and round, and down and down, deeper and deeper, and deeper into the warm, wonderful, welcoming valley, the beautiful, purple, dark, valley, the valley of relaxation.

You are not falling into that valley, you are in control; you are not falling as a stone, bouncing down and down and down until in the end it reaches the bottom of the valley, there to remain, never to return to the top of its own free will. No, you are in control, and you know you could, if you so wished, soar upwards out of the valley, up and up and up, to the snow-capped, sun-kissed peaks way above. But for now, you are content, on those wonderful wings of yours, to circle round and round, down and down, and deeper, deeper, deeper yet into that wonderful valley of relaxation.

Now you see below you the colours of the valley; the different greens of the grasses and the leaves on the trees; the bright plumes of the birds in the branches; the pastel shades of the flowers on the bushes, and the white of falling water.

And deeper and deeper down you go. Now you can hear the sounds of the valley; the sound of the breeze in the leaves of the trees, the sweet songs of the birds, and, away in the distance, the dull roar of falling water.

And down, down, down you go; now you smell the scents of the valley, the sharp scent of crushed herbs, the delicate scent of the flowers, the scent of the rich, damp, dark earth.

And down, down, down you go.... Now you can feel with your fingertips the different textures of the valley; how smooth it is, how rough it is, the velvety feel of the flower petals, the gentle caress of the mist that surrounds the falling water.

And deeper and deeper and deeper you go; down and down and down you go. And now you are able to pluck and to taste the fruit of the valley, the fruit which, as you taste it, tastes exactly like your own favourite fruit; so that, from now, whenever you taste that favourite fruit of yours, whatever it may be, you'll feel that you are crossing through the valley, feel the peace of the valley, that relaxation.

So now, going down and down, moving deeper and deeper into that wonderful, purple darkness, you feel coming up to meet you from the greater depths below you, the power of love, which, as it reaches you, it embraces you, wraps you around as if you were in a cocoon.

And, as the warmth increases, you become aware that you are allowing it to draw you down and down, deeper and deeper, down towards the very centre of that wonderful, purple darkness, that purple darkness of inner space which is the centre of yourself, the centre from which you are created and had your inner birth, the physical place where once was the single, fertilised cell from which we all start; and that flow of warmth, which the inner self sends out to draw you to itself, is the warmth of love that yourself has for you .

We all of us have heard words to the effect that we should love our neighbours as we love ourselves, and that supposes, of course, that we love ourselves before we can love our neighbours.

So you love yourself, and know that your self reciprocates, sends back that love multiplied a hundred times; that WARMTH OF LOVE not only wraps you round, but now is flowing through, flowing through every part of you, and now into every corner of your being.

Now as the warmth of love goes on drawing you to the centre, the self sends out to meet you A FLOW OF HEALING POWER. And the purpose of that love is to integrate you with the self, and that healing power creates the necessary unity, the wholeness and the harmony within you that releases all tensions and unties all knots; and then the energy can flow freely through, washing clean all unwanted aspects that are no further use to you.

And that healing power, like the warmth of love, flows through every part of you, flows into every corner of your being.

Together with the warmth of love and the healing power that flows to you from the self, there is a third quality that pervades the whole of your being; that third quality is THE WISDOM OF YOUR INNER SELF, which is your own, inborn knowledge and understanding, belonging to life itself.

That inner self of yours, of course, knows and understands everything about you, all your problems and difficulties, all your potentialities and creativities, all that has ever happened to you. Indeed, maybe it knows all that will ever happen to you, because it exists completely outside time as we normally know it; and that wisdom, like the healing power and the warmth of love, flows through you, fills every part of you, flows into every corner of your being, now.

Let yourself experience there three qualities - THE WARMTH OF LOVE, the HEALING POWER and THE WISDOM as they draw you into the care of the self in the centre of your being.

There you can rest, completely and totally, like a baby in its mother's arms, allowing the self to work on you, so that you may live your life in a way more appropriate to your present needs.

So now your body is deeply, deeply relaxed. As your body relaxes, so, of course, your mind relaxes too - the two go hand in hand. So, as your body relaxes, losing more and more of that inner - tension... so your mind relaxes too. And, as your body relaxed is a more efficient body, so your mind relaxed is clearer, keener calmer than before.

And being relaxed in body and calm in mind, you are at peace in your inner self and being, at peace in your inner self.

There's nothing in the past to worry about. The past has gone; it's left behind its memories and the lessons it taught you. But the past has gone; there's nothing in it to concern yourself with.

There's nothing in your future to be conscious about, because the future's not yet; and, when it arrives, it will be the present (a precious gift). And now, in the present, you know that the present holds no stress, no tension, no pressure, for you are in control. And being relaxed in body and calm in mind and at peace in your inner self, you are - and you will be - more confident, more confident in yourself, more confident in the things you do and in your success, more confident in your ability to cope with anything, with anybody, with any situation, with any problem no matter where you are or who you are with.

So now, as each day goes by, you will feel and you will become more and more physically relaxed; and that means it doesn't matter what your body is doing (whether it's lying or sitting, or standing; whether it's working or resting; still or moving, working or sleeping), it's using only the muscles and amount of energy necessary to carry out that particular function. The remainder of your body is relaxing; and in that way you are conserving energy, energy you can use in a whole lot of different ways; energy you can use to ENJOY LIFE.

So, as the days go by, you are feeling and becoming more physically relaxed; so you are feeling and becoming mentally calmer.

This means, of course, that your mind is crystal clear. Nothing and no one bothers you the same. I'm not saying, of course, that people and things won't annoy you (that would be asking too much) but nothing and no one can worry you in the same way as they did before. And, because your mind is clear and calm, you will find that it has stopped churning round and round unnecessarily; it has stopped worrying and started planning.

So, as the days go by, you feel and become physically relaxed, mentally clearer and calmer; so you will feel and become more and more at peace in your inner self. And being at peace in your inner self, the problems that you have been having are slipping away into the past where they really belong.

And as the problems slip away, it's just as though a weight has been lifted off you, allowing you to enjoy life more, and to be yourself more.

And so, as the days go by, and you are losing all trace of unnecessary tension in your head, your face, your neck, shoulders, arms and hands, your back, chest, abdomen, legs and feet, so you are leaving behind all unnecessary tension; so you find that you can cope with anything, with anybody, with any situation more and more and more easily.

As you find you can cope more easily with any situation, and as the days go by, you feel and you become more and more confident, as confidence is just the other three things put together; if you are relaxed in body, calm in mind and at peace in your inner self, so you are and will be more and more confident; able to be yourself, in control, more confident in yourself, more confident about whatever you are doing, more confident in your ability to cope with things and people; but ABOVE ALL, more confident in, and happier about, the future.

So here, now, you are and you will be more and more and more relaxed in body, mind and spirit.

To help you relax even more deeply than ever you have before, in a moment or two, I am going to say the word "NOW"; and when I say that word "NOW", I am going to stop talking (you will be surprised to hear) and when I say that word "NOW", I am going to stop talking for perhaps a minute, and during that time, you will allow yourself to relax even more deeply than you ever have before, and to do that, I am going to stop talking "NOW".

In a moment or two, our time together will be coming to an end, and so, in a moment or two, I shall count from 5 to 1. When I say the word "ONE", and not before, you will open your eyes in your own good time. And as you open your eyes, you will be back where you started from - it will be a little bit later, that's all. And when I say that word "ONE", and you open your eyes, when you open your eyes, you will feel so wonderfully relaxed in body, and so calm in mind, so much at peace in your inner self, so very, very confident. It will be as though a weight has been taken off you. You will feel absolutely wonderful. So ready,

5...4...3...2...1.

APPENDIX 3

VISUALISATION, THE MAGIC GARDEN
By Sue Washington

Approximately 15 minutes

This visualisation gives the unconscious mind a way of getting rid of things that are no longer valid or relevant in one's life. It is useful to use at the end of every day before going to sleep to get rid of irritations from the day. It is also useful to use it at this point to get rid of older, bigger issues.

THE MAGIC GARDEN

I want you to picture a garden in your mind's eye. I want you to make it an English Country Garden - with a high wall round the edge. Trees and creepers growing over the wall, tall flowers in front of it, smaller flowers in front of that and smaller still in front of that, right down to tiny flowers at your feet, all packed so closely together that you can hardly see any soil. The sun shining, the sky as blue as blue can be, and all around you, peace and calm and tranquillity. Feel the warmth of the sun on your head and on your back and smell the sweet scent of flowers all about.

There are insects too. Little buzzing things, big fat bees, pretty butterflies, and if you are very lucky, maybe even a dragonfly flying about, translucent wings and beautiful iridescent body. There are birds twittering about the place, with their coloured plumage and sweet songs: lawns, little paths, flowering shrubs, and somewhere water tinkling about the place....

I want you to go down to the bottom of the garden where the tall trees are. Tied to the tree with a big stout rope is a big balloon filled with lighter than air gas and swinging from the bottom of it, a large empty box, hovering four or six inches above the ground. It's a very special box. It can contain things that you want rid of. I want you to look around inside yourself and see if there's anything inside that you'd be better off without. You don't have to tell me what it is, not at all, but if there's anything in there you would be better off without, just NOD to let me know (wait for a nod). Fine. Take it, and push it out into the box and nod to tell me when you've done it (wait for a nod). (Repeat until there is nothing left. Wait for the participant's acknowledgement that they have finished).

Fine. I want you next to untie the big stout rope that holds down the balloon. The balloon will lift that box up, lighter and lighter, higher and higher. Higher and higher until it gets to the top of the tallest tree. Do you see that?

Lighter and lighter, higher and higher, until it is as small as the nail on your little finger.... Do you see that? Lighter and lighter, higher and higher until it disappears in a dot and the sky is clear. Eventually the balloon will burn up in the atmosphere and the contents of your box will frizzle away, getting rid of them like this will make you feel so much better.

Go back into the garden proper, and find yourself somewhere pleasant and peaceful to be ... just sit, or lie ... fill up the space inside yourself, with the good things that are around you, from where whatever it is, has left....

Because in a moment I'm going to count from one to three and say, "Open your eyes" and you're opening your eyes keeping that good feeling with you, so ready,

1...2...3... Open your eyes.

APPENDIX 4

This is printed out so that you can learn it as a visualisation. It is related to the visualisations you have on the CD – "The Magic Garden" and "The Three Dimensional Storage System". Please use the 'pictures' in the script printed below to heal yourself.

VISUALISATION - THE HEALING ROOM
By Sue Washington (with thanks to Betty Shine)

Approximately 15 minutes

I want you to picture a beautiful garden in your mind's eye. I want you to make it an English Country Garden - with a high wall round the edge. Trees and creepers growing over the wall, tall flowers in front of it, smaller flowers in front of that and smaller still in front of that, right down to tiny flowers at your feet, all packed so closely together that you can hardly see any soil. The sun shining, the sky as blue as blue can be, and all around you, peace and calm and tranquillity. Feel the warmth of the sun on your head and on your back and smell the sweet scent of flowers all about.

There are insects too. Little buzzing things, big fat bees, pretty butterflies, and if you are very lucky, maybe even a dragonfly flying about, translucent wings and beautiful iridescent body. There are birds twittering about the place, with their coloured plumage and sweet songs: lawns, little paths, flowering shrubs, and somewhere, water tinkling about the place ....

This time, I want you to go to the house that's over there in the corner. It's one of those houses that a child would draw, with a door in the middle and a window at each side - a big bay window in fact, and three windows across the top. It is a tall gracious, elegant house. The sun is shining full on the face of the house, and as you draw near the front door you can see things gleaming, the brass handle, the brass doorknob, the brass letterbox and the brass bell. The door isn't quite shut, and just as you're wondering whether to go in or not, you notice a little sticker underneath the door handle. "Welcome" with your name, it says.

Go on in. The hall is in front of you, painted in shades of lemon and white, and the stairs sweep up at the far end. All the doors down each side of the hall are closed, apart from the door immediately to your left, which seems to be the one you're meant to go into, so go on in, and close the door behind you for complete privacy. Lean on the back of the door to take stock of the room for a minute or two. The bay window is to your left overlooking the garden, and the sun is streaming in, making swirly patterns on the floor, and touching the edge of the table with the flower arrangement on it. Opposite you in the alcove is a bookcase, filled from floor to ceiling full of lovely, leather-bound identical books. Next to that, a marble fireplace with a rather nice picture hanging over it, and next to that in the other alcove shelves filled with interesting things.

This time, I want you to go over to the fireplace; it's beautifully carved in marble. As you're looking at it, you lean on a scroll. There's a quiet rumble, and, as if by magic, the bit underneath the fireplace rolls back, leaving the entrance to a secret room. You go in.

It's like an old fashioned alchemist's room. The walls are full of herbal products in jars, their colours looking lovely. Here is everything you could ever need to heal yourself, physically, intellectually, emotionally and spiritually. You go along the shelves, and again, as if by magic, you know exactly what to take, and how much... exactly what salve to rub into yourself. If there is anything lodged away that shouldn't be there, something prickly or barbed, then you know exactly how to tweak that out....

When you've done all that, lie and take a little rest. Fill yourself up with the special qualities of exceptional peace that are here.... All that you need to give you complete **Peace of Mind**....

The time you stay there can be as long as you want in your mind's time, but here in reality time it is only a minute or two...

Get up now and go out of the room, touching the spot on the fireplace that makes your room secret again. Go across the room into the hall. The front door's open, and the sun is streaming in to greet you. Find somewhere pleasant and peaceful to be for a few minutes.... Because I'm going to count from 1 to 7 and say the words "open your eyes", and you're opening your eyes feeling really good... no heaviness at all in any of your muscles, they're feeling so much better for the rest... You're opening your eyes with your mind crystal clear, and better than you've felt all day, so ready,

1...2...3...4...5...6...7... Open your eyes.

APPENDIX 5

VISUALISATION – THE THREE DIMENSIONAL STORAGE SYSTEM
By Sue Washington

Approximately 15 minutes

I want you to picture a garden in your mind's eye. I want you to make it an English Country Garden - with a high wall round the edge. Trees and creepers growing over the wall, tall flowers in front of it, smaller flowers in front of that and smaller still in front of that, right down to tiny flowers at your feet, all packed so closely together that you can hardly see any soil. The sun shining, the sky as blue as blue can be, and all around you, peace and calm and tranquillity. Feel the warmth of the sun on your head and on your back and smell the sweet scent of flowers all about.

There are insects too. Little buzzing things, big fat bees, pretty butterflies, and if you are very lucky, maybe even a dragonfly flying about, translucent wings and beautiful iridescent body.   There are birds twittering about the place, with their coloured plumage and sweet songs: lawns, little paths, flowering shrubs, and somewhere water tinkling about the place....

This time, I want you to go to the house that's over there in the corner. It's one of those houses that a child would draw, with a door in the middle and a window at each side - a big bay window in fact, and three windows across the top. It is a tall gracious, elegant house. The sun is shining full on the face of the house, and as you draw near the front door you can see things gleaming, the brass handle, the brass doorknob, the brass letterbox and the brass bell. The door isn't quite shut, and just as you're wonder wondering whether to go in or not, you notice a little sticker underneath the door handle "Welcome" with your name written next to it. it says.

Go on in. The hall is in front of you, painted in shades of lemon and white, and the stairs sweep up at the far end. All the doors down each side of the hall are closed, apart from the door immediately to your left, which seems to be the one you're meant to go into. So go on in, and close the door behind you for complete privacy. Lean on the back of the door to take stock of the room for a minute or two.   The bay window is to your left overlooking the garden, and the sun is streaming in, making swirly patterns on the floor, and touching the edge of the table with the flower arrangement on it. Opposite you in the alcove is a bookcase, filled from floor to ceiling full of lovely, leather-bound identical books. Next to that, a marble fireplace with a rather nice picture hanging over it, and next to that in the other alcove shelves filled with interesting things.

In front of the shelves is a desk, and behind the desk in front of the shelves, a chair, one of those that swivel round. Go and sit on the chair behind the desk. In front of you is a heap of white typing paper.

• Take a moment and look around inside your mind to find something that is on your mind, but something you know that you don't have to deal with immediately. Make some representation of that on the paper with the writing implement that's there, and let me know when you've done that. Fold your paper in four and put it to the side of the heap of paper. •

(Repeat between the two dots above until there is nothing left).

In a minute, I'm going to ask you to swivel around on you chair towards the shelves. You will find in front of you an attractive box with a tight fitting lid. OK, do that now, and pick up the box and bring it back to the desk. Remove the tight fitting lid, and place safely in there your stack of folded papers. Put the lid back on, and swing around to place the box back on the shelves. Look at the box, and make the mental promise to yourself to return and re-trace your steps back to this safe place, when you need to deal with the thing you've put in the box that is nearest in time to you. That time could be later on today, at Christmas, the start of the New Year or many years hence. The choice is yours.

Go out of the room into the hall. The front door is wide open, and the sun streaming in to greet you. Go on out in the garden, and find yourself somewhere pleasant and peaceful to be. Soak the beautiful things into yourself from around you, filling up the space where those other things have temporarily left. When you have done that, and keeping that good feeling with you, you can open your eyes.

APPENDIX 6

SOLUTION TO EXERCISE 15, SELF LIMITATION / EXPANSION

You were asked the following:

1. Join together the nine dots with four straight lines.

2. You must not double back on yourself.

3. You must not lift the pen off the paper.

Did you limit yourself to working inside the six dots, which is the commonest mistake? The correct solution is down below.

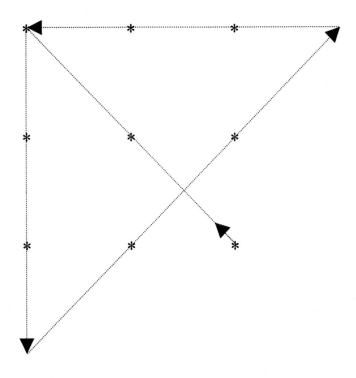

APPENDIX 7

REALISING the "SMALL PEACE" BETWEEN PARENTS and

CHILDREN – 10 POINTS OF VIEW

Based on Thomas Gordon's "Parents Effectiveness Training"

1. Being a parent is one of the most rewarding, but also one of the most difficult jobs, for which one does not get an education, as one gets for any other job.

2. Many problems between parents and children arise because of inadequate communication. Effective communication can be learned.

3. Children / teenagers do not rebel against parents, they rebel against the power parents use.

4. Education is possible with the use of little or no power, but with the use of respect for each other.

5. To be a good parent it is necessary to know yourself and your own needs.

6. To be a good parent it is necessary to know your child and his/her needs.

7. Feelings are facts! Both for parent and child.

8. Conflicts prevented between parents and children can be solved by (or prevented) by a problem-solving method. Nobody looses, everybody wins.

9. To be a good Quaker parent may be more difficult because of the high ideals Quakers have; the chance of disappointment / failure is for both parent and child.

10. It is fun to learn to be a better parent!

APPENDIX 8

This is not referred to in your text; however, I have included it from the Liverpool John Moore's programme as it is funny, but also raises the serious point of how much pressure is on parents these days! You will be able to 'chunk' up or down, I am sure, to find a parallel for you!

WANTED ADVERTISMENT

WANTED - A responsible person, male or female, to undertake a lifelong project. Candidates should be totally committed, willing to work up to 24 hours daily, including weekends during the initial 16 year period. Occasional holidays possible, but may be cancelled at no notice. Knowledge of health care, nutrition, psychology, child development, household management and the education system essential. Necessary: stress management and conflict resolution, negotiation and problem solving, communication and listening, budgeting and time management, decision making, ability to set boundaries and priorities as well as providing loving support. Necessary qualities: energy, tolerance, patience, good self-esteem, self-confidence and a sense of humour. No training or experience needed. No salary but very rewarding work for the right person.

APPENDIX 9

This is not referred to in your text; however, I have included it from the Liverpool John Moore's programme as it is funny, but also raises the serious point of how much pressure is on workers these days! You will be able to 'chunk' up or down, I am sure, to find a parallel for you!

THE GOSPEL ACCORDING TO SAINT DOROTHY

This "Gospel" was spotted on an office wall in Lancashire, England, and is used with the kind permission of the authors.

1.   Thou shalt be at thy desk at 8.58 a.m. precisely.

2.   Thou shalt not move from thy designated area of labour during the "working day" despite flood, war, famine, pestilence, fire, earthquake, suffocation due to paperwork or any other act of Dorothy.

3.   Thou shalt not interrupt Dorothy's working day, although thine may be interrupted at any time.

4.   Thou shalt meet all demands yesterday, despite not being in possession of the relevant information until tomorrow.

5.   Thou shalt achieve the miraculous without complaint.

6.   Thou shalt not automatically assume the role of terrified victim when commands are left on the answer-phone.

7.   Thou shalt automatically interpret stages 1-5 of an idea, despite being presented with the idea at stage 6.

8.   Thou shalt constantly strive to develop thy psychic abilities to keep up with the level of mind reading required.

9.   Thou shalt communicate the entire contents of Dorothy's idea to all staff involved whilst being in possession of only 5% of the whole.

10. Thou art not allowed to have a nervous breakdown without prior notification in triplicate.

11. Thou shalt tactfully ignore Dorothy's assertion that thou hast been asked for information when in reality thou has not. Thou shalt resourcefully create a solution, and when in doubt call a meeting.

12. Thou art required to photocopy every single piece of paper that thou intendeth to pass to Dorothy, so that when it is 'special filed' thou canst instantly provide the said information when it is demanded. (This simple precaution shalt prevent unnecessary scrabbling in bins).

13. Thou shalt understand the brilliance of Dorothy's mind, the speed of her thoughts and forgive her memory distortion when she 'remembers' a conversation.

14. Thou shalt always remember that thy job description includes the clause. "And any other duties deemed necessary by Dorothy".

From the loyal, devoted, knackered and affectionate serfs.

APPENDIX 10

This is not referred to in your text; however, I have included it from the Liverpool John Moore's programme. It is food for thought.

A GIFT TO YOU

"Peace is an internal matter, it must begin with your own thoughts, and then extend outwards."

(A Course in Miracles)

A GIFT TO YOU

"When a brother behaves insanely you can heal him only by perceiving sanity in him."

(A Course in Miracles)

BIBLIOGRAPHY

Bandler, R. & Grinder, J. (1979) <u>Frogs into Princes</u>. Eden Grove Editions

Bandler R. & Grinder J. (1981) <u>Trance-formations.</u> Real People Press

Bandler, R. & Grinder J. (1982) <u>Reframing: Neuro-Linguistic Programming and theTransformation of Meaning</u> Moab, Utah, Real People Press

Berne, E. (1959) <u>Principles of Group Treatment.</u> Grove.

Campbell, J., Moyers, B., (1988) <u>The Power of Myth</u>, Anchor Doubleday, New York.

Coué, E. (1922) Self Mastery Through Autosuggestion" (publisher unknown)

Corkille-Briggs, D., (1975) <u>Your child's self esteem</u>. Dolphin Books.

Csikszentmihalyi, M., (1992) <u>Flow - The Psychology of Happiness</u>. Harper & Row, London.

Davis, B., (1982) <u>The Magical Child Within</u>, Celestial Arts,

Dalley, S. (1998) <u>Myths from Mesopotamia: Creation, the Flood, Gilgamesh and Others</u>, Oxford World's Classics.

Ebrahim, D. W., (1970). Private tutorial, Chester UK.

Ellis, A. (1994). <u>Reason and Emotion in Psychotherapy</u>, (revised and updated). New York: Birch Lane Press book.

Galsworthy, J. (1906) <u>The Forsyte Saga</u> (available London, Penguin)

Gordon, T., (2000) <u>Parent Effectiveness Training: The Proven Program for Raising Responsible Children</u>. USA (CA), Three Rivers Press.

Hay, L., (1991) <u>The Power is Within You</u>, Eden Grove,

Hartland, Dr J.,(1966) <u>Medical and Dental Hypnosis</u> Bailliere Tindall.

Hewitt, J., (1992) <u>Teach yourself Meditation</u> Hodder, London.

Janov, A. (1973) <u>Primal Scream: Primal Therapy - the Cure for Neurosis,</u> Garnstone

Jung, C.G. (1995) <u>Memories, Dreams, Reflections,</u> Fontana Press; New Ed.

Kalff, D. (2000) Sandspiel. Reinhardt Ernst

Maslow, A. H., (1983) Religions: Values and Peak Experiences. USA; Smith.

Matthews, A. (1998) Being <u>Happy</u> Media Masters

Mehrabian, A., (1969) quoted in <u>Nonverbal Communication</u>, (2007) Aldine Transaction.

Montessori, M., in Lillard, P. P., (1988) <u>Montessori: A Modern Approach,</u> Kuperard; New Ed edition.

Moyers, B. (1988) <u>T Power of Myth</u> Anchor Doubleday, New York.

Rogers, C.R. (1942) <u>Counselling and Psychotherapy.</u> Houghton Miflin, Boston, MA.

Rogers, C.R. (1951) <u>Client-Centred Therapy: Its Current Practice, Implications and Theory</u>. Constable; London.

Rogers, C.R. (1957) '<u>The necessary and sufficient conditions of therapeutic personality change,</u> *Journal of Counseling Psychology,21; 95-103.*

Russell, W. (1988) <u>Shirley Valentine</u>, New Longman Literature.

Lankton, S., (1980) Practical <u>Magic</u>. Meta Publications.

Pease, A., & Pease, B., (2005) <u>Body Language: How to Read Others' Attitudes by Their Gestures</u>. Orion; New Ed edition.

Mehrabian, A., (1972) <u>Nonverbal Communication</u>. Walter De Gruyter Inc.

Scott Peck, M., (1988) <u>The Different Drum: Community Making and Peace</u>: UK, London, Rider.

Scott Peck, M., (1988) The Road less travelled UK; London. Rider.

Rogers, C. R., (2004) On Becoming a Person, Constable and Robinson; New Ed. edition

Shine, B. (1990) Mind to Mind: The Power and Practice of Healing, Corgi, London

Syer, J., & Connolly, C. (1988) Sporting Body, Sporting Mind: An Athlete's Guide to Mental Training. Prentice Hall Trade

Silva, J. & Stone, R.B., (1989) You the Healer: The World-Famous Silva Method on How to Heal Yourself and Others. HJ Kramer Inc.

Steiner, R., (1998) Gates of Knowledge USA; New York, Kessinger Publishing Co.

Wilde, S. (1987) Affirmations, Australia; NSW. Nacson & Sons Pty Ltd.

Washington S. (1994) Peace of Mind Manual, UK., Preston, Peace of Mind Training Limited.

Waxman D. (1981) Hartland's Medical and Dental Hypnosis UK: London, Bailliere Tindall.

Wilde, S. (1987) Affirmations, Nacson & Sons Pty Ltd, New South Wales, Australia

Willens, H., (1984) The Trimtab Factor: How Executives can help solve the Nuclear Weapons Crisis :USA, New York, William Morrow Company.

Winnicott, D. W., (1991) The Child, the Family and the Outside World UK. London, Penguin.

Zdenek, M., (1983) The Right Brain Experience, UK, London, Corgi.

Lightning Source UK Ltd.
Milton Keynes UK
UKOW03f1111300415

250636UK00001B/23/P